Legal Notice

Copyright Protected. All Rights
No part of this publication may be reproduced, distrib
any means, electronic or physical including photocopy
the prior written consent of MMCVisions Publishing a
except in the case of brief quotations embodied in critical reviews
noncommercial uses permitted by copyright law.

Title: THE CANDLESTICK PATTERN PLAYBOOK

Volume 2 of the Day Trading series

Author: The Million-Dollar Margin Club MMCVisions

Printed Version ISBN: 979-8-9890300-2-6

Publisher: MMCVisions Publishing

Publication Date: December 2023

For permission requests, contact: MMCVisions@gmail.com

Website: million-dollar-marginclub.com

Disclaimer: The information provided in this trading guide, chart pattern workbook is for entertainment and educational purposes only and should not be construed as financial or investment advice. You should conduct your own research and consult with a licensed financial advisor before making any investment decisions based on the content of this book. Trading securities involves risk and you could lose all or a portion of your investment. Do not follow the guidelines in this book until they have worked for you in a trading simulator and you have followed the advice of a licensed professional. By reading this book the reader agrees to hold the author harmless and not responsible for any losses incurred directly or indirectly from any and all the information contained in this book including, but not limited to, any strategies, errors, omissions, tools, layouts, studies, indicators or inaccuracies contained within.

The Million-Dollar Margin Club™

MMCVisions Publishing

Other Books by MMCVisions Publishing Available on Amazon

Welcome to DAY TRADING
A Complete Beginner's Guide and Workbook for Day Trading Using the RV Strategy

- Complete guidelines on how to trade the RV Strategy
- Details on how to open your first account with helpful suggestions of brokerages within the U.S. and offshore
- Learn studies and indicators
- The Million-dollar Margin Club's daily stock rating system
- Learn the importance of stock scanners
- 10 candlestick patterns rated for accuracy
- Learn range-bound channel trading and identifying support and resistance levels
- How stock consolidation can bring profits
- Create a day trading plan with a new way to manage risk
- 10 Things to remember when range-bound trading
- Advanced guidelines to understanding your own trade analysis
- Details on executing trades with chart examples from professional traders
- Importance of controlling your emotions while day trading
- Learn details on how to trade with Fibonacci Retracements, VWAP, SMA, EMA, RSI, Volume Profile, ADX, Level II, Time and Sales, and ATR
- Worksheets and logs with examples provided

10 Candlestick Patterns and The Ratings you Must Know Before you Trade

82% Accurate

When Identified, Bear flags will continue a trend an average of 82% of the time.

DAY TRADING VOL 1: Make a Living Day Trading   Million-Dollar Margin Club

DAY TRADING VOL 1

Finally a Complete Step by Step Guide on How to Day Trade and Scalp Using a Range Bound Strategy

Make a Living Day Trading

The Million-Dollar Margin Club's Beginners' RV Strategy

"Candlestick Mastery Beginner to Pro in 66 Patterns" is an engaging guide that hones your technical analysis skills through a series of hands-on exercises. With challenges ranging from recognizing named candlestick patterns to predicting their direction, this book offers a dynamic learning experience, culminating in the ultimate test of naming the patterns.

Challenges Include:

- Beginner: Find the Named Candlestick Patterns
- Advanced: Find and Name the Candlestick Patterns
- Expert: Name and Predict the Direction of the Candlestick Pattern
- Professional: Name the Candlestick Patterns

Course and Study Guide for "The Candlestick Pattern Playbook"

Candlestick Mastery Beginner to Pro in 66 Patterns

DAY TRADING VOL 3

Learn Technical Analysis with Charts and Challenges

Candlestick Mastery Beginner to Pro in 66 Patterns

17th century Munehisa Homma contemplates his next trade

This image provided by John Bull Bear historical archives was created shortly after the disastrous abacus accident that cost Munehisa his ring finger. Some believe the accident caused the mathematical error that triggered the catastrophic rice shortage of 1687 which resulted in many citizens losing their life savings.

DAY TRADING VOL 3

Other Books by MMCVisions Publishing Available on Amazon

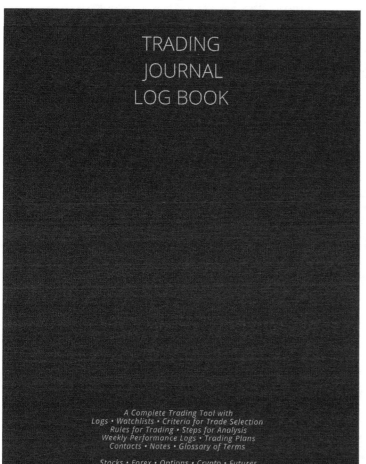

Other Books by MMCVisions Publishing Available on Amazon

CRYPTO TRADING LOGBOOK AND JOURNAL
TRADE LIKE A PROFESSIONAL

THE MILLION-DOLLAR MARGIN CLUB SHARES 4 TRADERS' PROFITABLE STRATEGIES USED IN WORLDWIDE COMPETITION

STOCK TRADING LOGBOOK AND JOURNAL
TRADE LIKE A PROFESSIONAL

THE MILLION-DOLLAR MARGIN CLUB SHARES 4 TRADERS' PROFITABLE STRATEGIES USED IN WORLDWIDE COMPETITION

PENNY STOCK TRADING LOGBOOK AND JOURNAL
TRADE LIKE A PROFESSIONAL

THE MILLION-DOLLAR MARGIN CLUB SHARES 4 TRADERS' PROFITABLE STRATEGIES USED IN WORLDWIDE COMPETITION

FOREX TRADING LOGBOOK AND JOURNAL
TRADE LIKE A PROFESSIONAL

THE MILLION-DOLLAR MARGIN CLUB SHARES 4 TRADERS' PROFITABLE STRATEGIES USED IN WORLDWIDE COMPETITION

TABLE OF CONTENTS

Chapter 1 .... Page 1
- Origin of the Candlestick • Importance of Candlestick Patterns
- Candlestick Patterns Used with Different Trading Styles
- A Basic Candlestick • Candlestick Rating System

Chapter 2 .... Page 9
- Most Common Candlestick Patterns Looked for by Day Traders and Scalpers, Including Their Accuracy Ratings

Chapter 3 .... Page 45
- Other Unique Candlestick Patterns Looked for by Day Traders and Scalpers, Including their Accuracy Ratings

Chapter 4 .... Page 63
- Quizzes: Try and Find the Hidden Patterns within the Charts

Chapter 5 .... Page 89
- Quiz Answers to the Hidden Patterns

Chapter 6 .... Page 121
- Have fun as you learn Your Candlestick Patterns with These Helpful Flashcards

STEP BY STEP HOW TO LEARN CANDLESTICK PATTERNS

THE CANDLESTICK PATTERN PLAYBOOK can help you to learn and memorize candlestick patterns. Many traders believe understanding candlestick patterns can be the key to any trader's success. Identifying these patterns in the moment can help traders decide when to enter or exit a position.

Most traders watch multiple indicators when day trading or scalping and must make very fast desisions based on their technical analysis of all these indicators.

THE CANDLESTICK PATTERN PLAYBOOK contains tools to help you remember all the patterns of the candlesticks so they can become muscle memories with little to no delay in identifying these patterns, allowing you to act quickly to capitalize on the most predictable movements of the security.

Chapter 1 Candlestick patterns are considered, by many, to be the **most important** indicator to help predict the future direction of a security. Reacting to these patterns very quickly can be the key to any trader's success. Understanding the anatomy of a basic candlestick is essential when analyzing candlestick patterns.

Chapter 2 The most common and recognized patterns for day trading. It is extremely important to learn these patterns completely, so you can act at a moments notice while trading.

The rating system is an added bonus to help with the validity and accuracy of each pattern. Some would argue that the percentage of accuracy for a candlestick pattern isn't as important as it is to act on the pattern itself and be prepared to exit if it is not confirmed. The accuracy rating can be an aid in deciding the entry share size of a trade. Most importantly as a trader, you need to be able to identify all these patterns quickly as they can affect your entry and exit in a longer-term strategy.

Chapter 3 Once you memorize chapter 2, learning the less common patterns in chapter 3 can add to your trading success.

Chapter 4 Identify the most important candlestick patterns in larger chart time frames. Completing these quizzes is important so you can learn to see these patterns in a real context.

Chapter 5 Continue to test yourself with the candlestick patterns highlighted within the chart puzzles with an ultimate goal of 100% accuracy.

Chapter 6 includes the important tools you will need for memorization. The **Flashcards** included in this chapter are meant to be cut out and laminated, if possible. This will ensure they will hold up as you constantly test yourself or work with another trader so both can learn. This method has been used by many day traders and can be a fun game to play with others as you learn.

Special Thanks to the Million-Dollar Margin Club's Book Review and Editing Team's newest member: Dwayne Price

If you would like to join the book review and editing program and get advanced access to the newest Million-Dollar Margin Club's books
Email: MMCVisions@gmail.com
Include the subject line: "Join the MMC"

CHAPTER 1

- **The Origin of the Candlestick**
- **The Importance of Patterns**
- **Candlestick Pattern's Trading Styles**
- **A Basic Candlestick**
- **Candlestick Rating System**

The Origin of the Candlestick

To understand the origin of candlestick patterns, we must embark on a journey back in time to ancient Japan. During the 17th century a legendary rice trader named Munehisa Homma, developed a revolutionary method of analyzing price action. Homma observed that emotions and market psychology played a crucial role in determining price movements, a concept far ahead of its time.

Homma's revolutionary insights led to the development of the first primitive form of candlestick charting, which employed a series of vertical lines resembling candlesticks. These candlesticks depicted the open, high, low, and close prices for a specific time period. This groundbreaking visual representation of price action gained popularity and laid the foundation for what would later become known as candlestick patterns.

Originally in trading, there were 9 identified candlestick "patterns" including: Marubozu, Doji, Hammer, Shooting Star, Spinning Top, Hanging Man, Engulfing Pattern, Dark Cloud Cover, and Piercing Pattern. The first 6 of these are single candlesticks and the last 3 are multiple candlestick patterns.

The 20th century witnessed the gradual adoption of candlestick patterns by Western Traders and investors. Notably, in the 1930's, a financial journalist named Charles Dow incorporated the principles of candlestick analysis into his Dow Theory, which laid the foundation for modern technical analysis. This integration helped bridge the gap between Eastern and Western trading methodologies, leading to further refinement and wider acceptance of candlestick patterns.

Now, with the advent of computer technology, pattern recognition in candlestick charts has become more accurate and efficient by using advanced algorithms to identify patterns automatically and quickly. Candlestick patterns can readily be tracked across multiple time frames to increase the accuracy of predictions. Candlestick patterns can be used in conjunction with other technical indicators such as moving averages, volume analysis, and trend lines. Quantitative analysis is made easier, leading to the development of statistical models that quantify the probabilities associated with candlestick patterns.

Candlesticks and candlestick patterns have a rich history and have evolved over time. From their origins in 17th-century Japan to their widespread use in modern technical analysis, they have become an integral part of traders' toolkits. In today's fast-paced day trading markets, identifying and reacting to specific candlestick patterns rapidly can help assure a trader's success.

The Importance of Candlestick Patterns in Trading

Candlestick patterns are an essential tool in technical analysis for traders looking to make informed decisions in the financial markets. These patterns provide visual representations of price action, indicating shifts in market sentiment and potential trading opportunities. When applied to intraday trading, candlestick patterns can help identify short-term trends, reversals, and entry/exit points.

Candlestick patterns are formed by a combination of multiple candlesticks, each representing a specific time interval. The open, close, high, and low prices of each interval are depicted through the body and wicks/shadows of the candlestick. By analyzing the relationships between these prices, traders can gain insights into market dynamics.

In intraday trading, where timeframes are relatively short, these charts provide detailed information about price movements within each interval. Traders can observe candlestick patterns forming in real-time and utilize them to make rapid trading decisions. When trading intraday it is crucial to understand candlestick patterns as they form so you can anticipate their continuation or reversal. Each pattern carries a specific meaning and can signal different market scenarios. Traders should look for patterns that align with their trading strategies and confirmations from other technical indicators. It's important to note that relying solely on candlestick patterns without additional analysis may lead to false signals.

Some momentum traders will use a chart with a short time frame, such as a one-minute chart, and often focus on patterns that provide timely insights. As the chart displays each minute's price action, it is possible to spot candlestick patterns forming. Traders often take advantage of these patterns by identifying potential entry and exit points for quick trades.

Often day traders will use a five-minute chart, which gives them more time to analyze patterns and make decisions. The patterns formed on this time frame may provide more reliable signals compared to the one-minute chart. Traders can still identify patterns quickly, but they may carry more weight due to the extended time frame. It is crucial to remain patient and not rush into trades solely based on one candlestick pattern. Regardless of the time frame, some common candlestick patterns include reversal patterns, continuation patterns, and indecision patterns. Reversal patterns signal potential trend reversals, while continuation patterns suggest the current trend is likely to continue. Indecision patterns often indicate a period of consolidation or market uncertainty.

When a candlestick pattern is identified, traders can use it to inform their trading decisions. For example, if a reversal pattern is recognized, such as a bullish engulfing pattern, it may indicate a potential bullish reversal. Traders could consider entering a long position or closing existing short positions, expecting the price to rise. However, it's important to wait for confirmation from subsequent candlesticks or other indicators before taking action.

Candlestick Patterns used with Different Trading Styles

Long-Term Trading focuses on capturing significant price movements over weeks, months, or even years. Candlestick patterns can play a crucial role in analyzing the market behavior of long-term trading and providing insights into potential reversals, continuations, and trend confirmations. These patterns often offer clear signals and can provide valuable information for making informed long-term trading decisions. Some patterns that fall into this category include Marubozu, Hammer, Inverted Hammer, Engulfing, Bull Flag, and Morning Star.

Swing Trading is a style that aims to capture larger price swings over a few days to several weeks. Candlestick patterns are an important part of swing trading, providing valuable insights into market behavior and aiding in the identification of potential trend reversals, continuations, or breakouts. A Morning Star pattern that occurs at the end of a downtrend, indicates a potential bullish reversal, making it valuable for swing traders looking for early indications of trend shifts.

Hammer and Inverted Hammer, characterized by small bodies and long shadows, suggest potential bullish reversals. Head and Shoulders, a long-term reversal pattern consisting of distinct peaks and troughs, is also well-suited for swing trading. It indicates potential trend reversals and can help traders identify optimal entry or exit points.

Day Trading is a fast-paced intraday trading style that requires quick decision-making and capitalizing on short-term movements. Candlestick patterns are invaluable tools for day traders, providing insights into market behavior and aiding in the identification of profitable trading opportunities. As with any trading style, some candlestick patterns work better than others. Patterns that work best for day trading are those that offer clear and immediate signals, allowing traders to make rapid trading decisions. These patterns often indicate potential trend reversals, breakouts, or continuations, enabling day traders to capitalize on short-term price movements. Examples of patterns that work well for day trading include Engulfing, Morning Star, Hammer, Inverted Hammer, Bull Flag, Shooting Star, Bear Flag, Tweezer, and Head and Shoulders patterns.

Scalping is a popular short-term trading approach characterized by multiple quick trades throughout the day, aiming to capture small price differentials. In scalp trading, speed and precision are essential and traders rely on candlestick patterns that offer immediate signals and facilitate swift decision-making. Candlestick patterns play a vital role in scalping, providing valuable insights into market behavior and giving visual assistance in finding potential reversals, breakouts, or short-term price movements. Scalping is reliant on quick candlestick reading and has a tendency to use smaller patterns unlike other forms of trading. Candlestick patterns that Scalping traders find useful include Engulfing, Hammer, Inverted Hammer, Doji, and Dragonfly.

This book has identified and rated 65 of the most useful candlestick patterns used in **day trading and scalping**. Many are shown within larger chart patterns to help with identification and memorization.

A Basic Candlestick

A basic candlestick represents the price action within a specific time frame, such as a minute, hour, or day. It consists of four main components: open, close, high, and low prices. The body of the candlestick represents the range between the open and close prices, while the wicks or shadows depict the high and low prices.

To trade a single candlestick on an intraday chart, it's important to consider the context and the specific type of candlestick formation. Different candlestick patterns provide insights into market sentiment and potential trading opportunities. For example, a bullish candlestick with a large body and small or nonexistent wicks suggests strong buying pressure. In this case, traders may consider entering a long position or holding onto existing long positions, anticipating further upward movement.

A bearish candlestick with a large body and minimal wicks indicates strong selling pressure. Traders might consider shorting the stock or closing existing long positions to take advantage of potential downward movement.

It is essential to remember that trading decisions should not rely solely on single candlestick formations. It's advisable to use candlestick patterns in conjuction with other indicators, such as moving averages, trendlines, and volume analysis, to confirm potential trade setups and manage risk effectively.

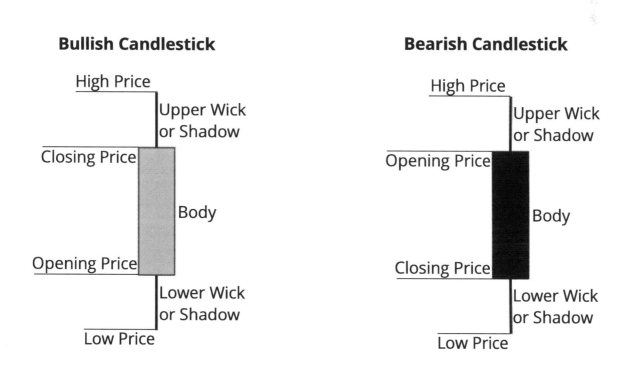

Candlestick Rating System

A new and innovative rating system has been developed by professional traders to enhance the precision and reliability of using candlestick patterns in stock price predictions. This system quantifies the accuracy of candlestick patterns through rigorous back testing and cross-comparison with similar rating systems. It is important to note the location of any given pattern within a larger pattern on a chart and that chart's specific time increment may affect the overall accuracy of the pattern's rating.

The rating system included here utilizes a comprehensive approach, including an extensive dataset of historical price movements. Many sources were used to research and compile this information.* A wide range of securities were evaluated, over time, that enabled a comprehensive analysis.

Within the historical data set, the rating system identifies and categorizes many diverse candlestick patterns, including well-known formations like Doji, Hammer, Engulfing, Shooting Star, Bull and Bear Flags. It's important to note, all the patterns rated with this system were analyzed using moderate to high volume within their proper trend. Our findings have shown that if a pattern is not identified within its proper trend it cannot be relied on to complete its pattern with any consistency. Some candlestick pattern rating analysis outcomes may differ if they do not rate a pattern within its proper alignment.

Sources: The Million-Dollar Margin Club, ChatGPT 4.0, Investopedia, Wikipedia, patternswizard.com, stockcharts.com, medium.com, alphaexcapital.com, quantifiedstrategies.com, liberatedstocktrader.com, etoro.com, investor.com, tradeciety.com, corporatefinanceinstitute.com, and the book DAY TRADING VOL 1 by MMCVisions

CHAPTER 2

- **Most Common Candlestick Patterns Including Their Accuracy Ratings Used by Day Traders, Scalpers, and Swing Traders**

"Like navigating a well thought-out plan, with every step in learning we measure points of progress; as we ascend in knowledge, we can chart our path to success."
- *John Bull Bear*

Bullish Marubozu Candlestick

Is characterized by a long body with no or minimal shadows, indicating a strong bullish sentiment. When it appears as a bullish candlestick pattern it can be a stong indicator of support for a reversal of a downtrend or continuation of an uptrend.

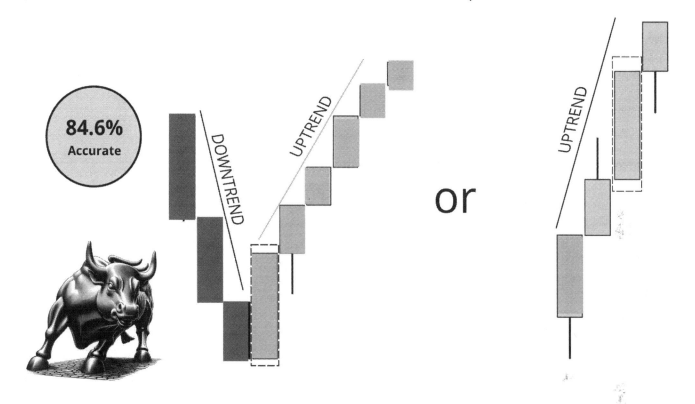

Chart Example of a Bullish Marubozu Candlestick

Bearish Marubozu Candlestick

Is characterized by a long body with no or minimal shadows, indicating a strong bearish sentiment. When it appears as a bearish candlestick pattern it can be a stong indicator of support for a reversal of an uptrend or continuation of a downtrend.

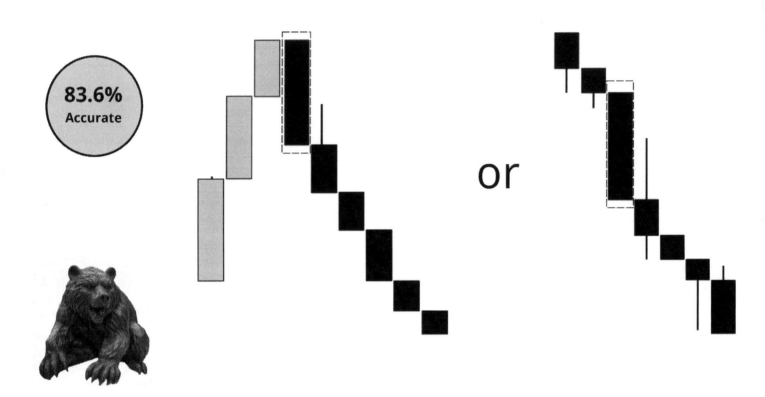

Chart Example of a Bearish Marubozu Candlestick

Graphics Provided by The Million-dollar Margin Club™

Hanging Man Candlestick

The lower wick is at least twice the length of the body. Appearing after an uptrend, it suggests a potential bearish reversal if confirmed by subsequent price action.

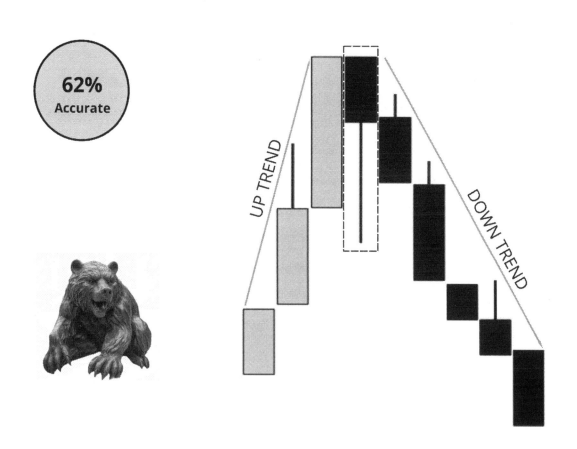

Chart Example of Hanging Man Candlestick

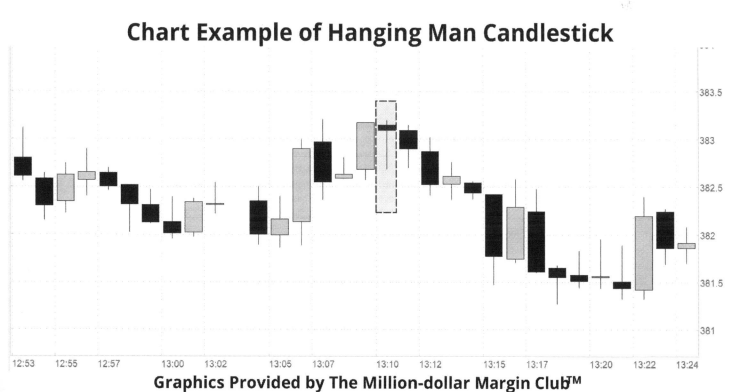

Graphics Provided by The Million-dollar Margin Club™

Hammer Candlestick

The lower wick is at least twice the length of the body, appearing after a downtrend. It suggests a potential bearish reversal if confirmed by subsequent price action.

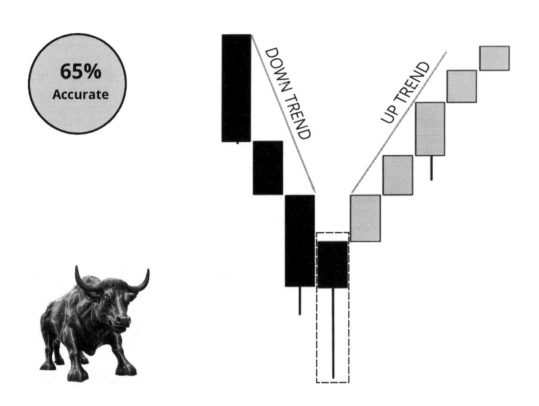

Chart Example of Hammer Candlestick

Graphics Provided by The Million-dollar Margin Club™

Shooting Star Candlestick

The upper wick is at least twice the length of the body. It appears after an uptrend and suggests a potential bearish reversal.

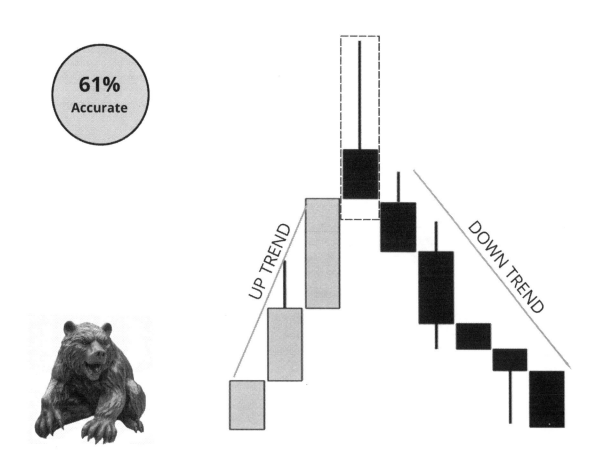

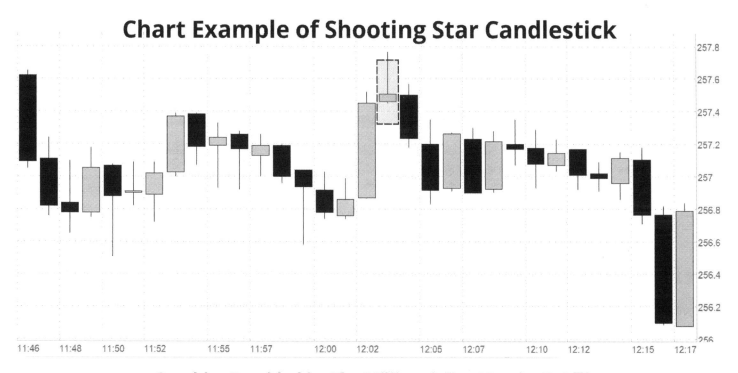

Chart Example of Shooting Star Candlestick

Graphics Provided by The Million-dollar Margin Club™

Inverted Hammer Candlestick

The upper wick is at least twice the length of the body. It appears after a downtrend and suggests a potential bullish reversal.

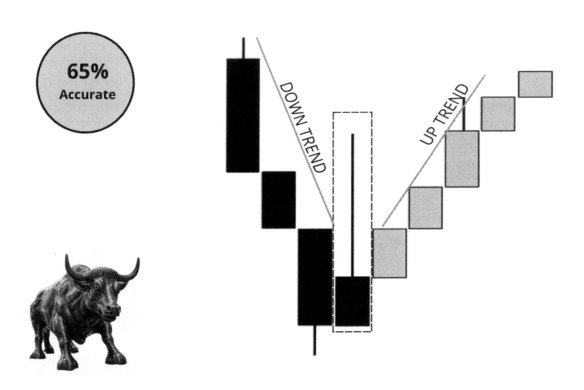

Chart Example of Inverted Hammer Candlestick

Doji Candlestick

Candlestick has a small Body, indicating that the opening and closing prices are very close or nearly the same. It represents market indecision and suggests a potential trend reversal. Traders look for confirmation from subsequent candlesticks to determine the direction of the next move.

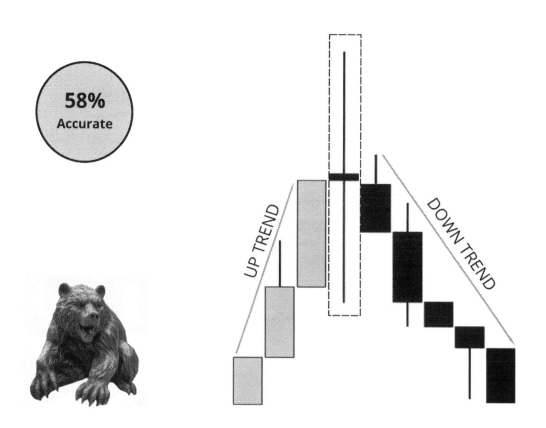

Chart Example of Doji Candlestick

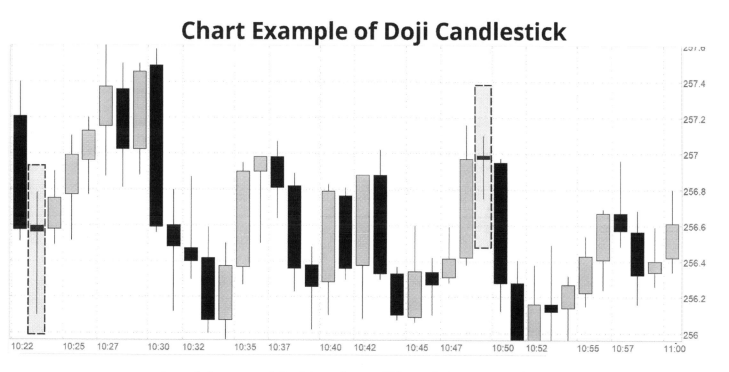

Graphics Provided by The Million-dollar Margin Club™

Dragonfly Candle

Is a pattern found in financial charts. It is characterized by a narrow opening and closing price, which creates a long lower shadow. The upper shadow is usually nonexistent or very short. This pattern resembles a dragonfly, with its body forming the thin line in the middle and the long shadow resembling its tail. The Dragonfly Doji suggests indecision in the market as buyers and sellers are in equilibrium. It often indicates a potential reversal in the price trend.

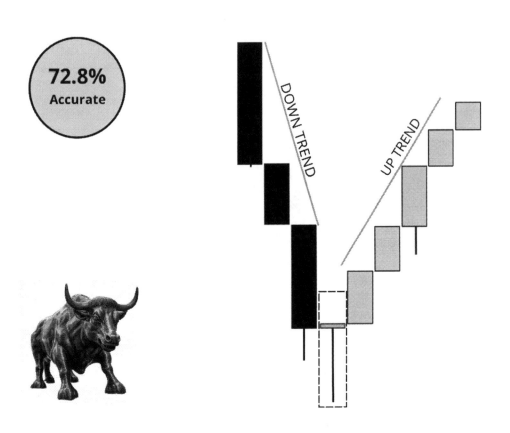

Chart Example of a Dragonfly Candlestick

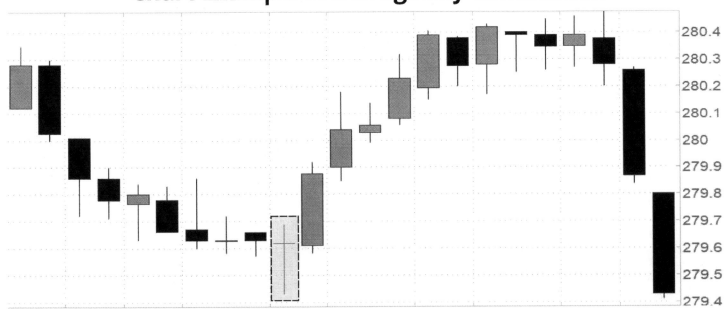

Graphics Provided by The Million-dollar Margin Club™

Gravestone Candle

Is observed in financial charts. It appears as a long upper shadow with little to no lower shadow, resembling a gravestone. The opening and closing price are near the low of the candle. This pattern indicates bearish sentiment in the market, suggesting a potential reversal from an uptrend to a downtrend. It signifies selling pressure and a possible shift in price direction.

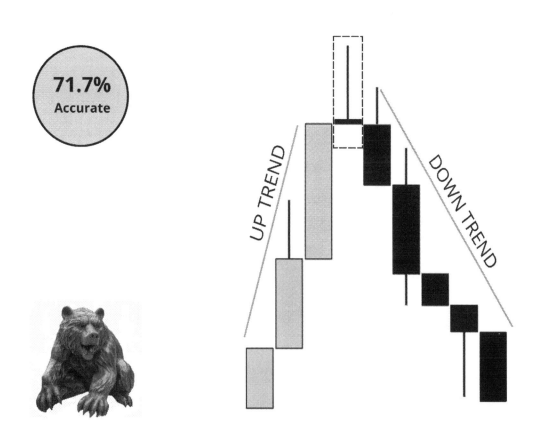

Chart Example of a Gravestone Candlestick

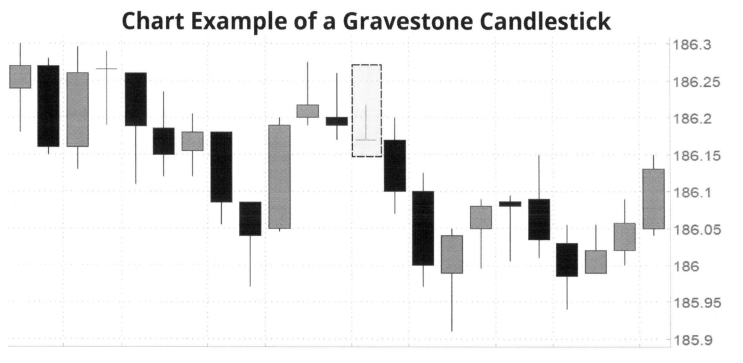

Graphics Provided by The Million-dollar Margin Club™

Bullish Engulfing Candlestick Pattern

Consists of two candlesticks and indicate a potential trend reversal. A Bullish Engulfing pattern occurs when a small bearish candlestick is followed by a larger bullish candlestick that completely engulfs the previous candlestick's body. It suggests a shift from bearish to bullish sentiment. Conversely, a Bearish Engulfing pattern occurs when a small bullish candlestick is followed by a larger bearish candlestick that engulfs the previous candlestick's body, indicating a potential shift from bullish to bearish sentement.

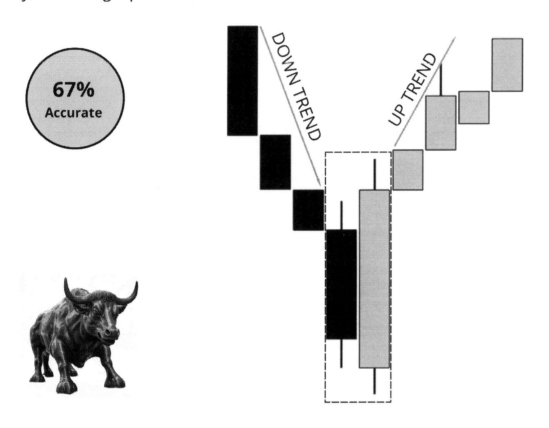

Chart Example of Bullish Engulfing Candlestick Pattern

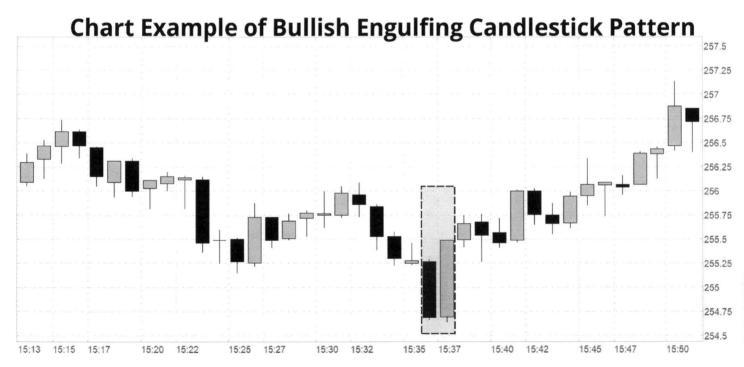

Graphics Provided by The Million-dollar Margin Club™

Bear Flag Candlestick Pattern

Occurs within a downtrend and is characterized by a sharp, steep decline in price (known as the flagpole) followed by a consolidation phase with lower volume and relative smaller price swings than the initial decline forming a rectangular or parallelgram shape know as the flag. To trade the bear flag pattern, traders may consider short-selling the stock when the price breaks below the lower support line of the flag, with a stop loss order placed just above the upper resistance line. Profit targets can be set by measuring the height of the flag pole and projecting it downward.

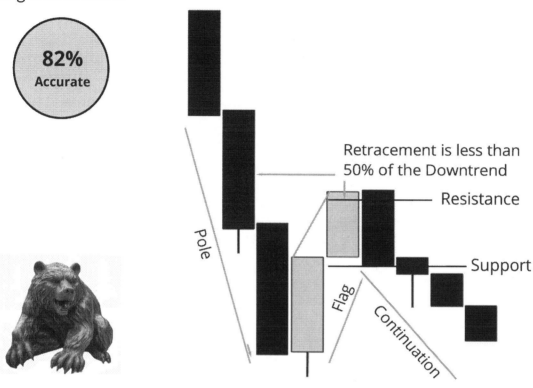

82% Accurate

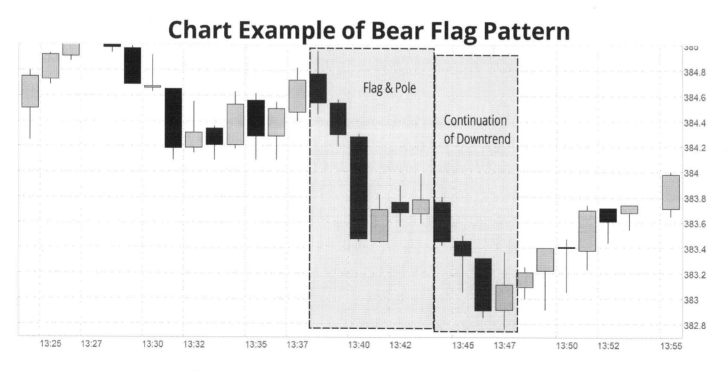

Chart Example of Bear Flag Pattern

Graphics Provided by The Million-dollar Margin Club™

Bull Flag Candlestick Pattern

Occurs within an uptrend and is characterized by a strong, steep upward move (the flagpole) followed by a consolidation phase of lower volume and relatively smaller price swings than the initial upward move forming a rectangular or parallelogram shape known as the flag.

To trade the bull flag pattern, traders may consider buying the stock when the price breaks above the upper resistance line of the flag, with a stop-loss order placed just below the lower support line. Profit targets can be set by measuring the height of the flagpole and projecting it upward from the break of the resistance line.

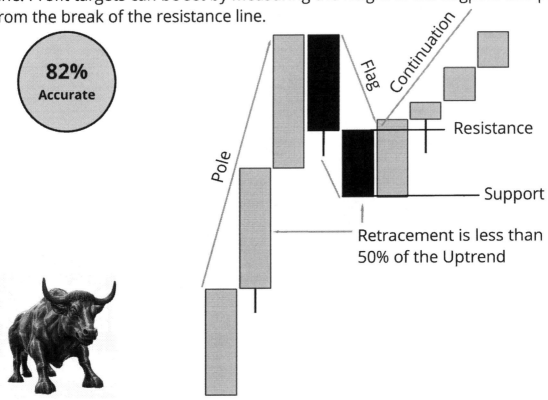

Chart Example of Bull Flag Pattern

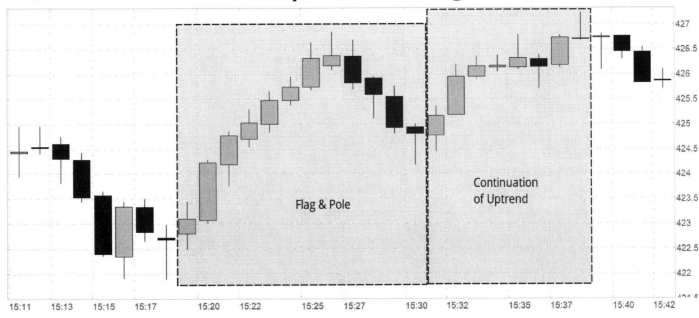

Graphics Provided by The Million-dollar Margin Club™

Head and Shoulders Candlestick Pattern

Is a reversal pattern that has three peaks and two troughs, where central peak (head) is taller than the left and right peaks (shoulders). It indicates potential downtrend if the candle breaks through the support (neck).

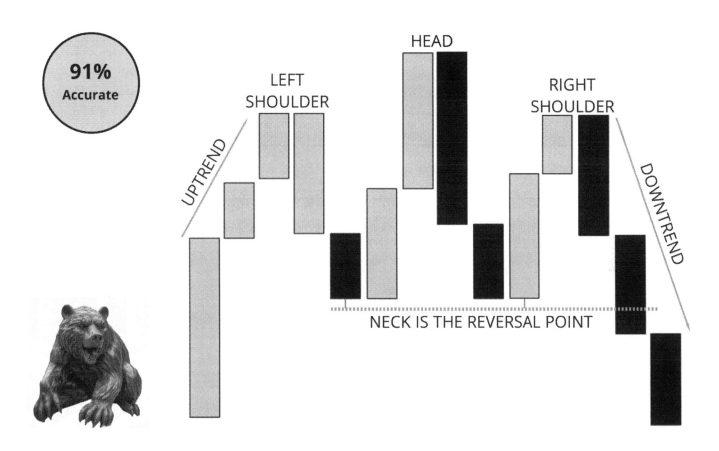

Chart Example of Head and Shoulders Pattern

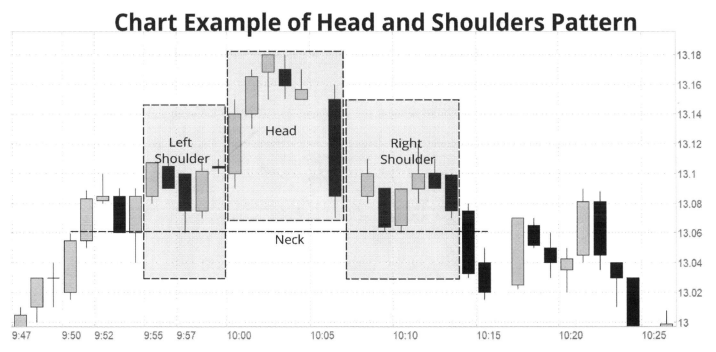

Graphics Provided by The Million-dollar Margin Club™

Break of Pre-Market High Candlestick Pattern

Occurs when a stock's price surpasses the highest level it reached during pre-market trading. This breakout often indicates increased buying interest and suggests potential strength for the trading day. Traders closely watch for the break of pre-market high as a signal to enter long positions, anticipating further upward movement and potentially capitalizing on the early momentum

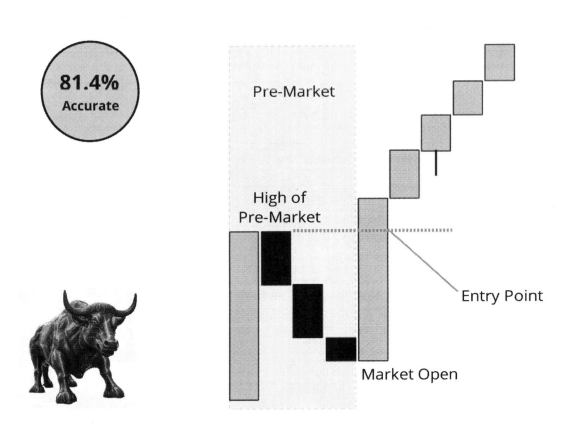

Chart Example of Break of Pre-market High Pattern

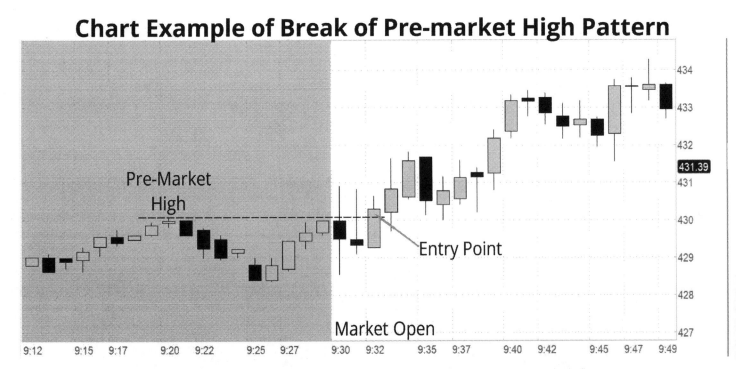

Graphics Provided by The Million-dollar Margin Club™

Flat Top Breakout Candlestick Pattern

A bullish pattern that occurs when a stock's price breaks through a horizontal resistance level that has been tested by multiple candles. It indicates a potential surge in buying pressure and the possibility of continued upward movement. Traders watch for flat top breakouts as they represent a significant breakout from a price range, capturing the attention of market participants seeking bullish opportunities and potential price increase.

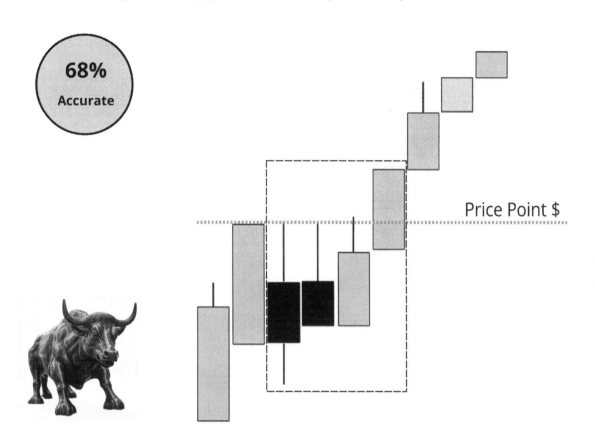

Chart Example of Flat Top Breakout Pattern

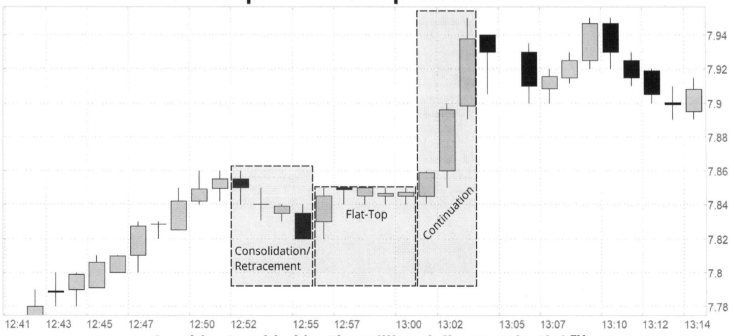

Graphics Provided by The Million-dollar Margin Club™

Evening Star Candlestick Pattern

Is a three-candlestick formation seen on stock charts. It begins with a bullish candle, followed by a small-bodied candle indicating indecision, and concludes with a bearish candle that closes below the midpoint of the first candle. This pattern signifies a potential reversal from an uptrend to a downtrend. It suggests a shift in market sentiment, with sellers gaining control and a possible decline in prices ahead.

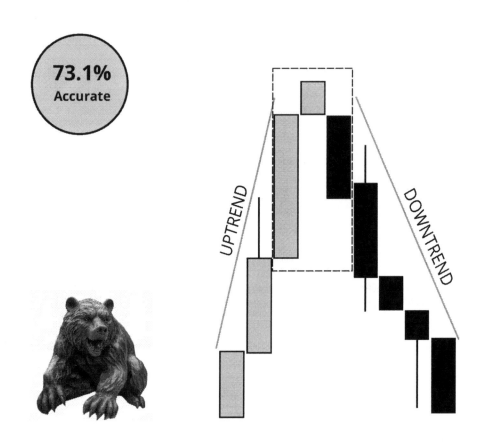

Chart Example of an Evening Star Pattern

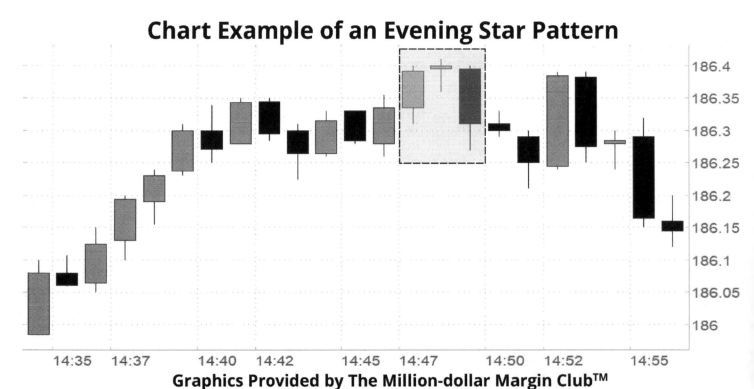

Graphics Provided by The Million-dollar Margin Club™

Morning Star Candlestick Pattern

Is a three-candlestick formation seen on stock charts. It begins with a bearish candle, followed by a small-bodied candle indicating indecision, and concludes with a bullish candle that closes above the midpoint of the first candle. This pattern signifies a potential reversal from a downtrend to an uptrend. It suggests a shift in market sentiment, with buyers gaining control and a possible increase in prices ahead.

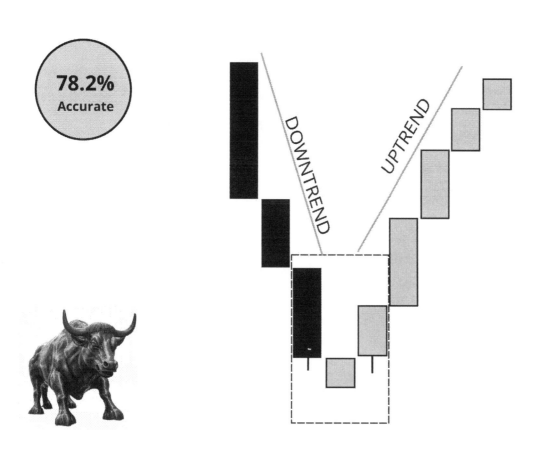

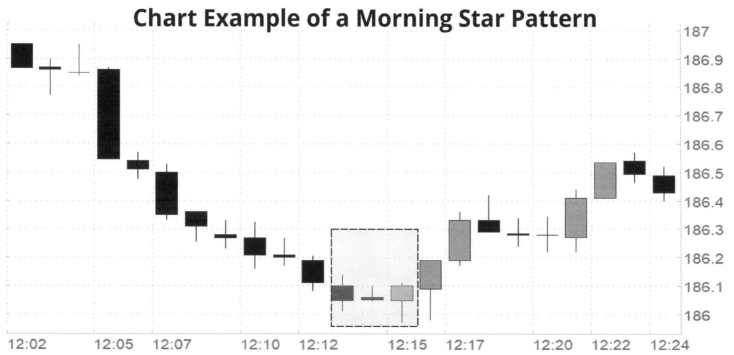

Chart Example of a Morning Star Pattern

Graphics Provided by The Million-dollar Margin Club™

Bearish Harami Candlestick Pattern

Is a two-candlestick formation on stock charts. It starts with a large bullish candle, followed by a smaller bearish candle that is completely engulfed by the previous candle's body. This pattern suggests a potential reversal from an uptrend to a downtrend. It indicates a decrease in buying pressure and a possible shift towards selling pressure. Traders often interpret it as a signal to consider short-selling or exiting long positions.

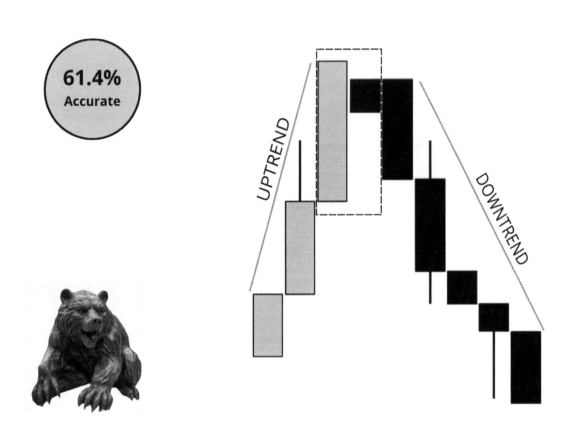

Chart Example of a Bearish Harami Pattern

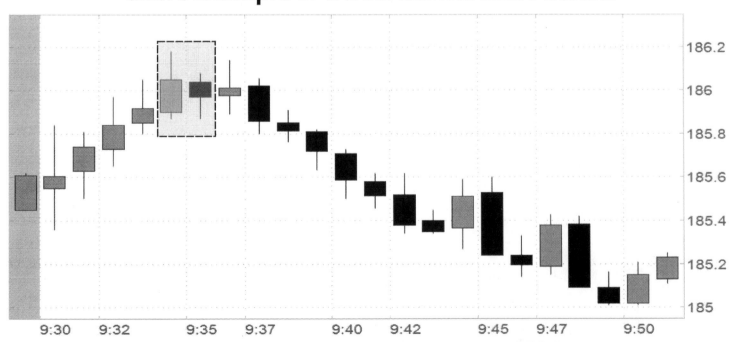

Graphics Provided by The Million-dollar Margin Club™

Bullish Harami Candlestick Pattern

Is a two-candlestick formation on stock charts. It starts with a large bearish candle, followed by a smaller bullish candle that is completely engulfed by the previous candle's body. . This pattern suggests a potential reversal from a downtrend to an uptrend. It indicates a decrease in selling pressure and a possible shift towards buying pressure. Traders often interpret it as a signal to consider entering a long position or exiting short positions.

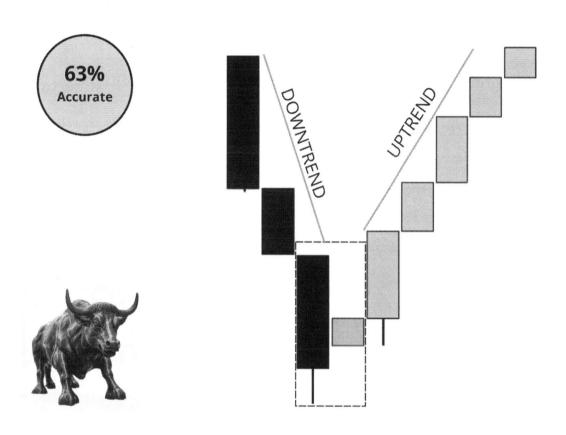

Chart Example of a Bullish Harami Pattern

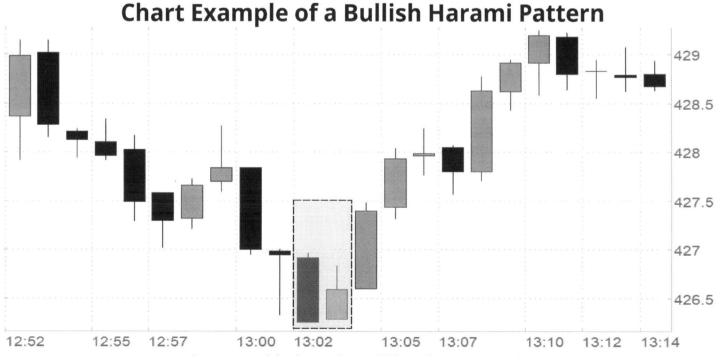

Graphics Provided by The Million-dollar Margin Club™

Bearish Tweezer Candlestick Pattern

Is a two-candlestick formation on stock charts. It consists of two consecutive candles with identical highs, indicating a resistance level. The first candle is bullish, while the second one is bearish, creating a tweezer-like shape. This pattern suggests a potential reversal from an uptrend to a downtrend. It signifies a shift in market sentiment, with selling pressure increasing and buyers losing momentum. Traders often interpret it as a signal to consider short-selling or exiting long positions.

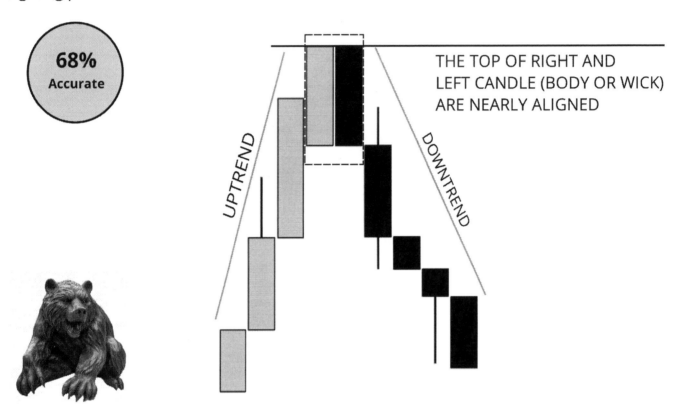

Chart Example of a Bearish Tweezer Pattern

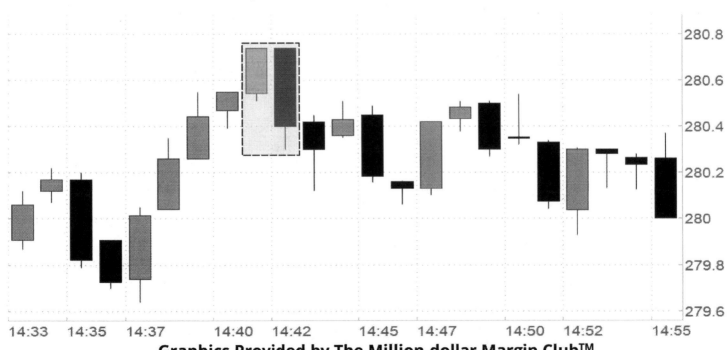

Graphics Provided by The Million-dollar Margin Club™

Bullish Tweezer Candlestick Pattern

Is a two-candlestick formation on stock charts. It consists of two consecutive candles with identical highs, indicating a resistance level. The first candle is bearish, while the second one is bullish, creating a tweezer-like shape. This pattern suggests a potential reversal from a downtrend to an uptrend. It signifies a shift in market sentiment, with buying pressure increasing and sellers losing momentum. Traders often interpret it as a signal to consider taking a long position or exiting short positions.

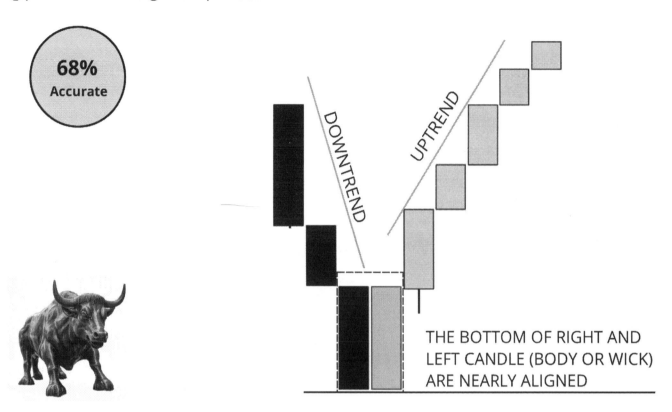

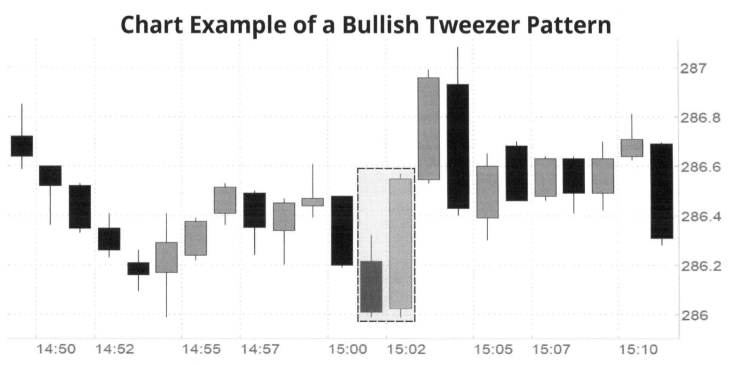

Graphics Provided by The Million-dollar Margin Club™

Three White Soldiers Candlestick Pattern

Is a bullish candlestick pattern. It consists of three consecutive bullish candles, each opening within the previous candle's body. Additionally, each candle closes near or at its high, indicating sustained buying pressure. This pattern suggests a potential trend reversal from bearish to bullish.

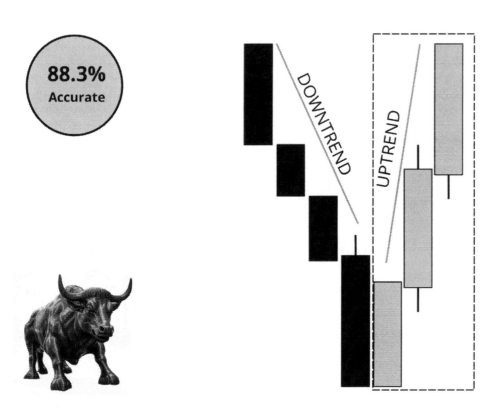

Chart Example of Three White Soldiers Pattern

Graphics Provided by The Million-dollar Margin Club™

Three Black Crows Candlestick Pattern

Is a bearish candlestick pattern. It consists of three consecutive bearish candles, each opening within the previous candle's body. Additionally, each candle closes near or at its low, indicating sustained selling pressure. This pattern suggests a potential trend reversal from bullish to bearish.

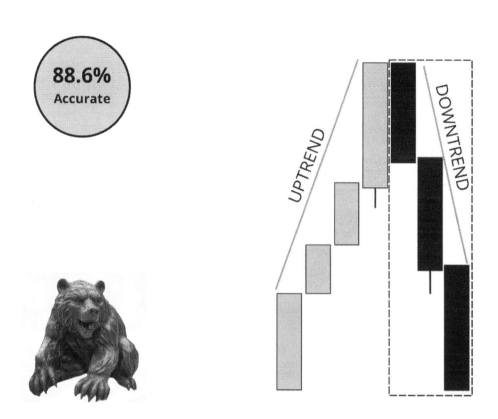

Chart Example of Three Black Crows Pattern

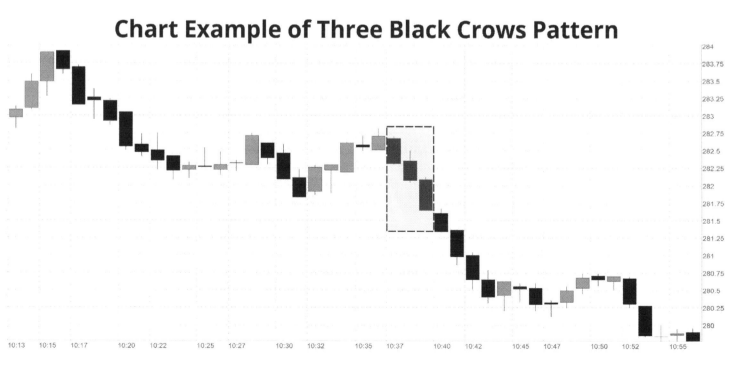

Graphics Provided by The Million-dollar Margin Club™

Dark Cloud Cover Candlestick Pattern

Occurs when a bullish candle is followed by a bearish candle that opens above the previous candles close and closes below its halfway point. This pattern suggests a potential trend reversal, signaling a bearish outlook and possible selling pressure in the market.

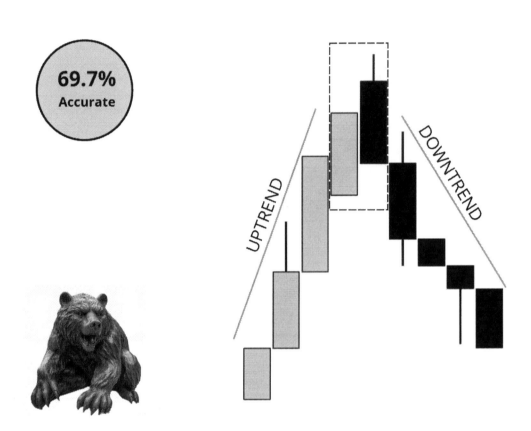

Chart Example of Dark Cloud Cover Pattern

Graphics Provided by The Million-dollar Margin Club™

Bearish Mat Hold Candlestick Pattern

Is identified by a long bearish candle followed by a bullish candle that opens within or below the previous candle and two more consecutive candles with higher lows and higher highs that do not pass the high of the first bearish candle, and finally a bearish candle that extends below the lows of the preceding bullish candles. It suggests a potential continuation of the bearish trend.

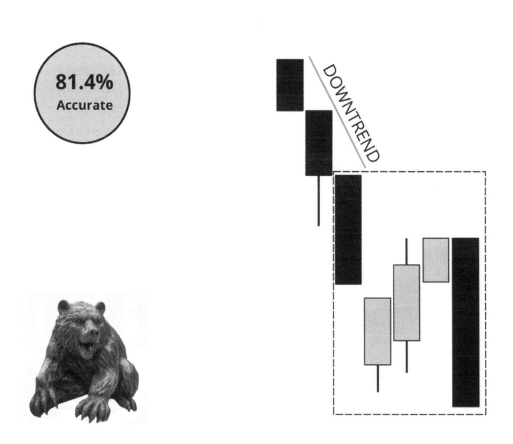

Chart Example of Bearish Mat Hold Candlestick Pattern

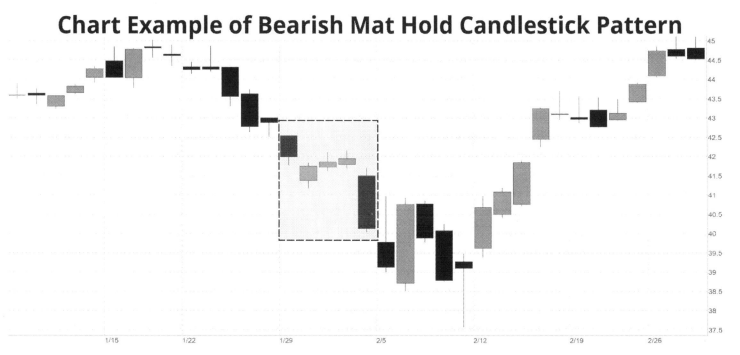

Graphics Provided by The Million-dollar Margin Club™

Bullish Mat Hold Candlestick Pattern

Is identified by a long bullish candle followed by a bearish candle that opens within or above the previous candle and two more consecutive candles with lower lows and lower highs that do not pass the low of the first bullish candle, and finally a bullish candle that extends above the highs of the preceding bearish candles. It suggests a potential continuation of the bullish trend.

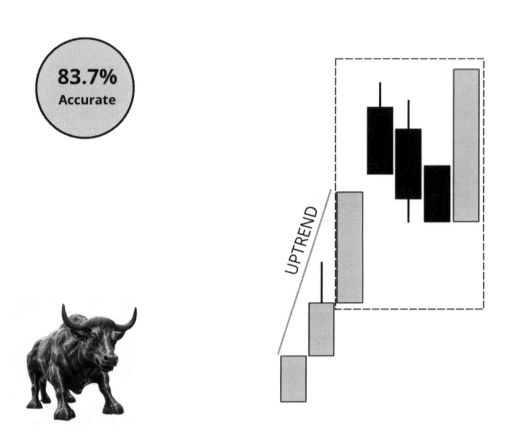

83.7% Accurate

Chart Example of Bullish Mat Hold Pattern

Graphics Provided by The Million-dollar Margin Club™

Rising Three Candlestick Pattern

Is formed by a long bullish candle followed by a series of three small-bodied bearish candles, each with lower lows and lower highs, that stay within the high-low range of the first candle, and finally a bullish candle that closes above the highs of the previous three candles. it signifies a potential continuation of the uptrend.

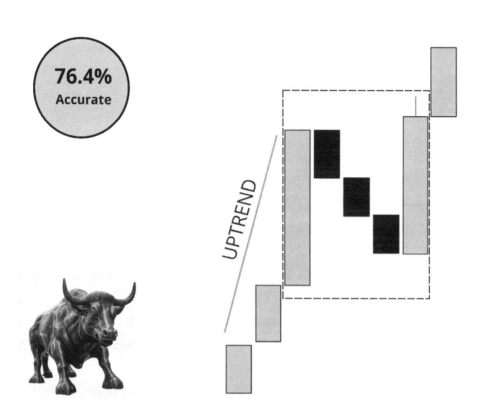

Chart Example of Rising Three Pattern

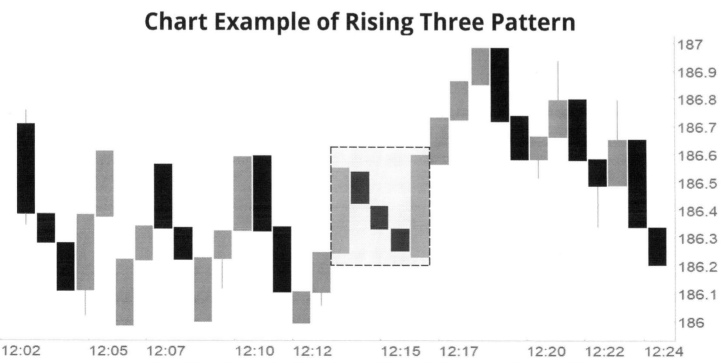

Graphics Provided by The Million-dollar Margin Club™

Falling Three Candlestick Pattern

Is characterized by a long bearish candle, followed by three small-bodied bullish candles that stay within the high-low range of the first candle, and finally, a bearish candle that closes below the lows of the previous three candles. It signifies a potential continuation of the trend.

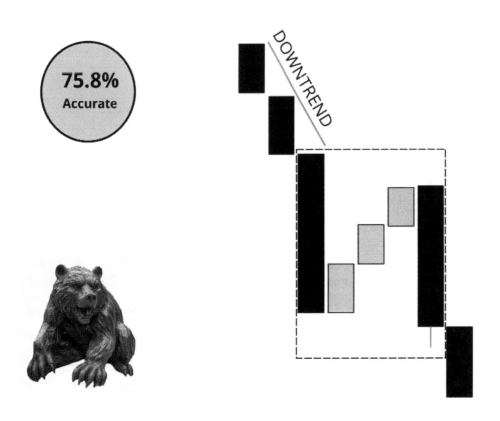

Chart Example of Falling Three Pattern

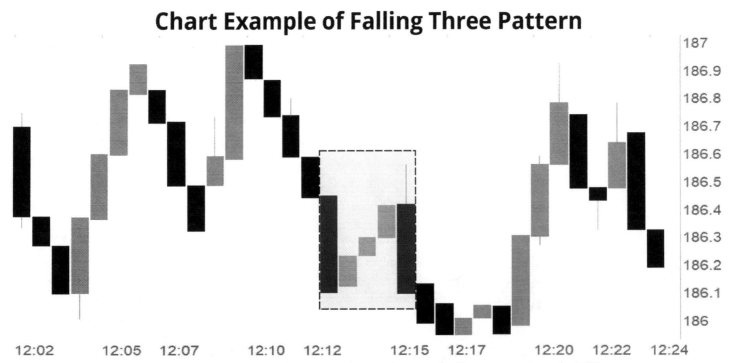

Graphics Provided by The Million-dollar Margin Club™

Ladder Top Candlestick Pattern

Is formed by a series of three consecutive bullish candles with higher highs and higher lows, resembling a ladder shape, then a smaller 4th bullish candle with a long lower shadow, and finally, a bearish candle that opens below the open of the previous candle. It signifies an uptrend losing momentum indicating potential exhaustion and a possible trend reversal. Traders often interpret it as a signal to be cautious and consider taking profits.

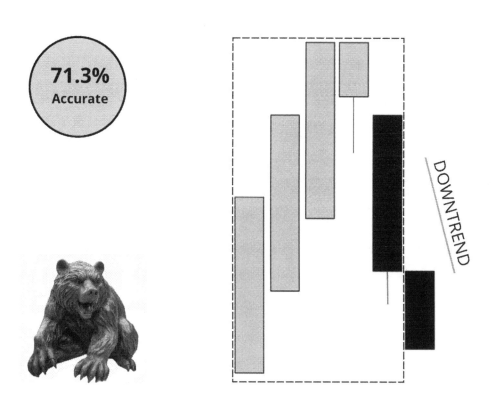

Chart Example of Ladder Top Pattern

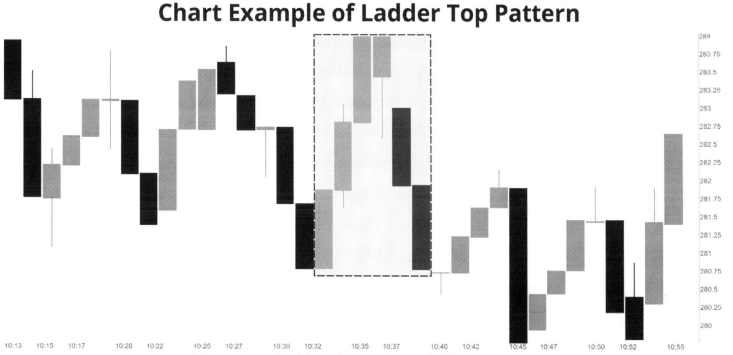

Graphics Provided by The Million-dollar Margin Club™

Ladder Bottom Candlestick Pattern

Is formed by three consecutive bearish candles with lower highs and lower lows, followed by a smaller bearish candle with a long upper shadow, and then a bullish candle that opens above the open of the previous candle. It indicates a weakening in the sellers trend and a potential reversal to an uptrend. Traders will look to enter a long position or exit short positions.

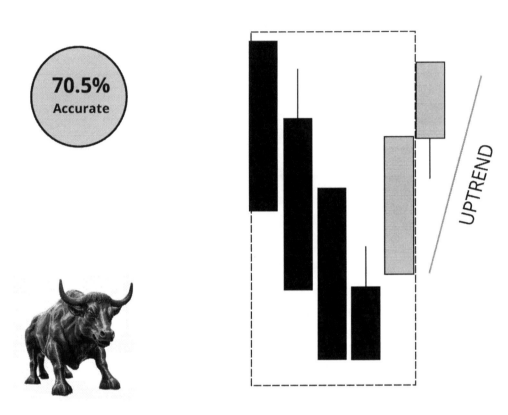

Chart Example Ladder Bottom Pattern

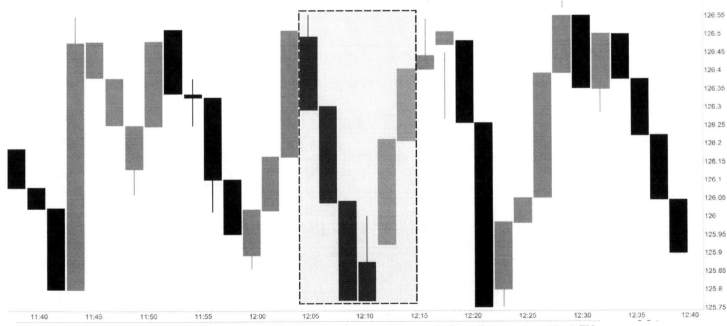

Graphics Provided by The Million-dollar Margin Club™

Bullish Abandoned Baby Candlestick Pattern

A three candle pattern. The first candle is a long bearish candle at the end of a downtrend. The 2nd candle gaps down from the 1st candle and forms a doji. The third, a long bullish candle, opens above the doji candle.

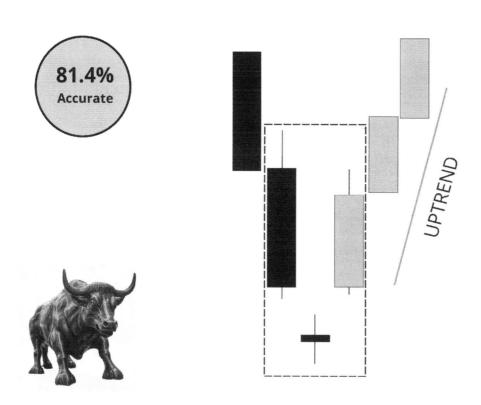

Chart Example Bullish Abandoned Baby Pattern

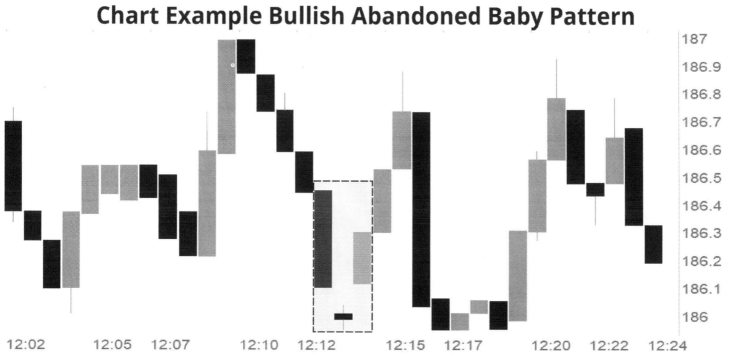

Bearish Abandoned Baby Candlestick Pattern

A three candle pattern. The first candle is a long bullish candle at the top of an uptrend. The 2nd candle gaps above from the 1st candle and forms a doji. The third, a long bearish candle, opens below the doji candle.

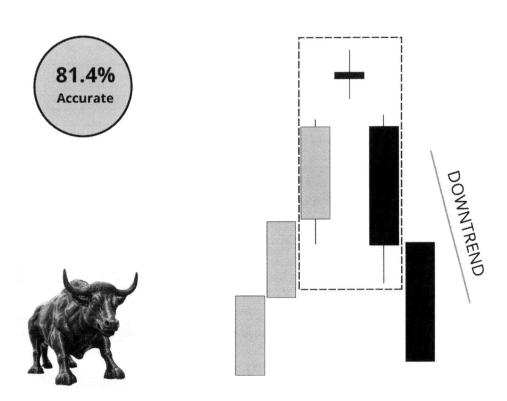

Chart Example Bearish Abandoned Baby Pattern

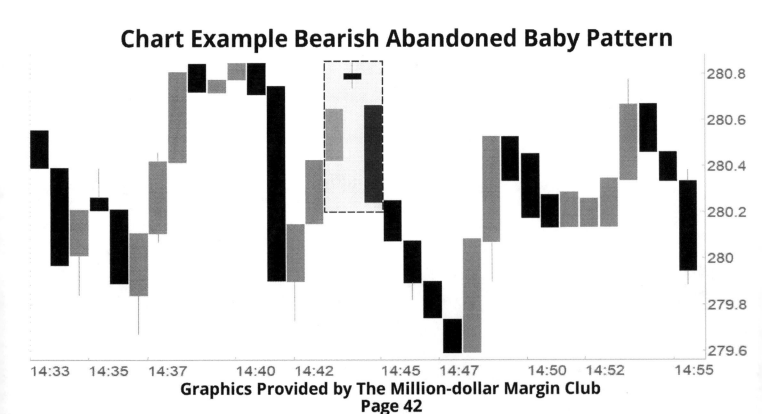

Graphics Provided by The Million-dollar Margin Club

Cup and Handle Candlestick Pattern

The Cup and Handle Candlestick Pattern is a found on daily, weekly, or monthly charts. The pattern is formed as a U or bowl shape is formed with lower volume as the candles form at the bottom of the bowl. The handle is a pullback of the finished cup.

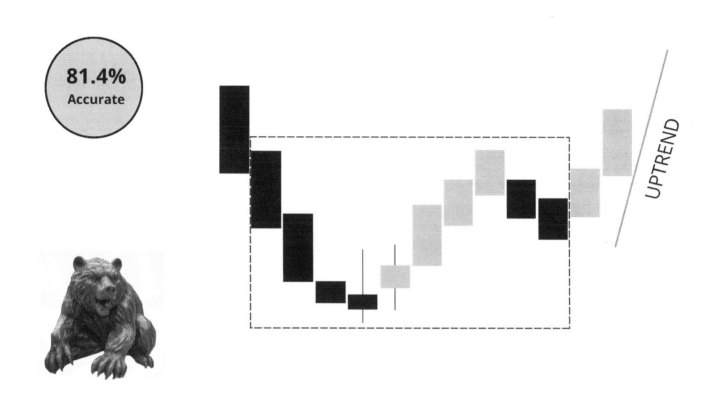

Chart Example Cup and Handle Pattern

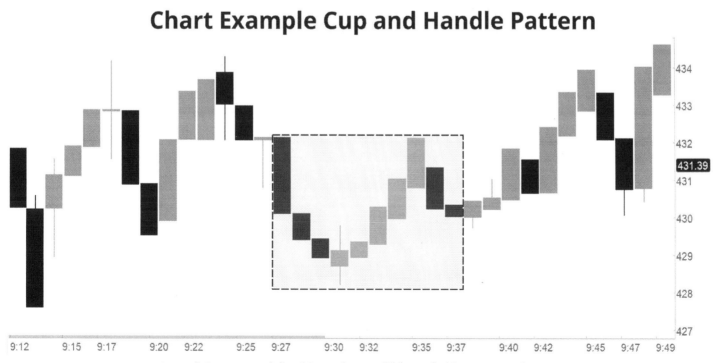

Graphics Provided by The Million-dollar Margin Club

CHAPTER 3

- **Other Unique Candlestick Patterns with Their Accuracy Ratings Used by Day Traders, Scalpers, and Swing Traders**

Bearish Hikkake Candlestick Pattern

A pattern formed by 5 candles. The first two candles are a Harami. The third candle closes above the high of the previous two candles. The fourth candle trades above the third candle. The final candle closes below the low of the second candle or even the first candle.

This is a Continuation Pattern

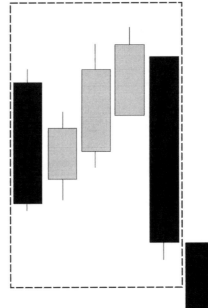

Bullish Hikkake Candlestick Pattern

A pattern formed by 5 candles. The first two candles are a Harami. The third candle closes above the high of the previous two candles. The fourth candle trades above the third candle. The final candle closes below the low of the second candle or even the first candle.

This is a Continuation Pattern

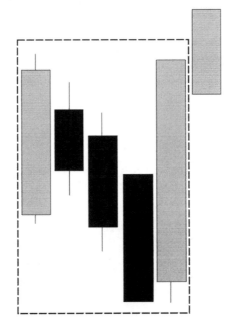

Bullish Separating Lines Candlestick Pattern

A two candle pattern consisting of a bearish candle followed by a bullish candle that opens at or near the same price point at which the bearish candle had opened.

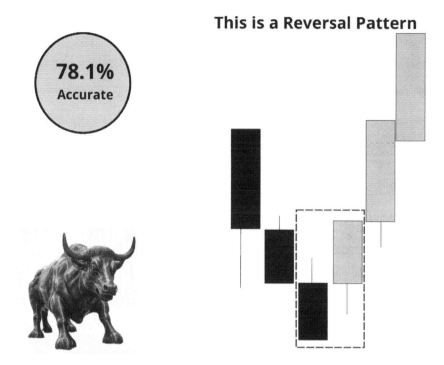

Bearish Separating Lines Candlestick Pattern

A two candle pattern consisting of a bullish candle followed by a bearish candle that opens at or near the same price point at which the bullish candle had opened.

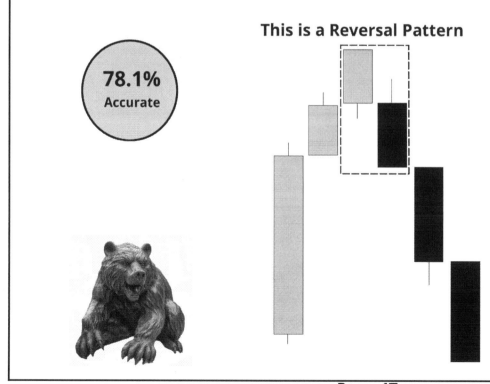

Three Inside Up Candlestick Pattern

A three candle pattern formed by a long bearish candle followed by a smaller candle that is enclosed between the open and close of the first candle and then a third candle that closes higher than the second candle.

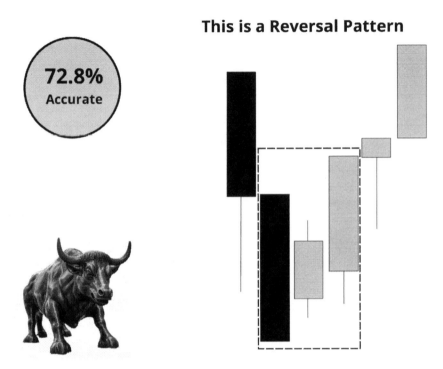

This is a Reversal Pattern

Three Inside Down Candlestick Pattern

A three candle pattern formed by a long bullish candle followed by a smaller candle that is enclosed between the open and close of the first candle and then a third candle that closes lower than the second candle.

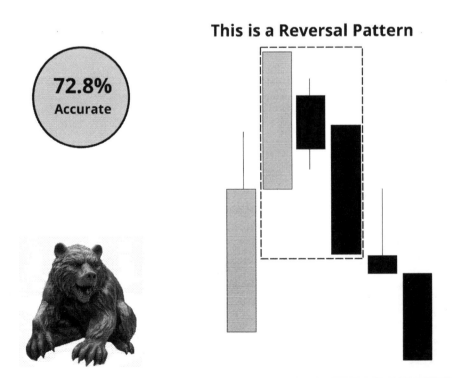

This is a Reversal Pattern

Bearish Three Line Strike Candlestick Pattern

A four candle pattern. The first candle is a long bearish candle followed by two bearish candles each opening between the previous candles opening and closing and closing below the previous candles closing. The fourth candle is a long bullish candle that closes above the first candles high.

This is a Continuation Pattern

69.4% Accurate

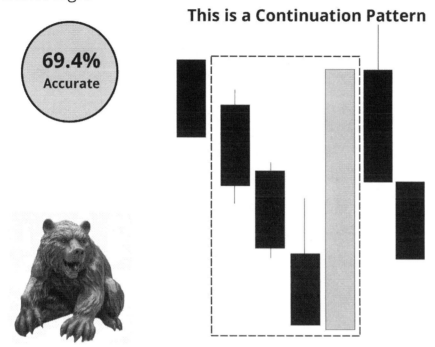

Bullish Three Line Strike Candlestick Pattern

A four candle pattern. The first candle is a long bullish candle followed by two bearish candles, each opening between the previous candles opening and closing and closing above the previous candles closing. The fourth candle is a long bearish candle that closes below the first candles low.

This is a Continuation Pattern

70.1% Accurate

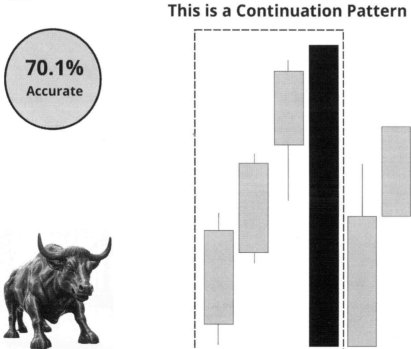

Three Outside Down Candlestick Pattern

A three candle pattern where the first two candles form a Bearish Engulfing candle and the third candle closes lower than the second candle.

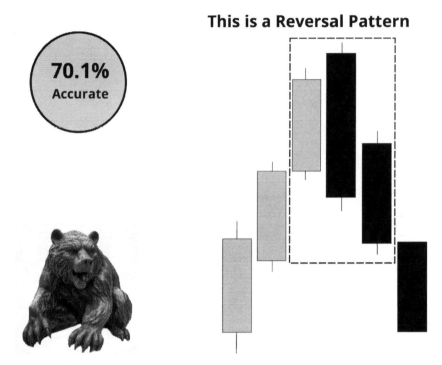

Three Outside Up Candlestick Pattern

A three candle pattern where the first two candles form a Bullish Engulfing candle and the third candle closes higher than the second candle.

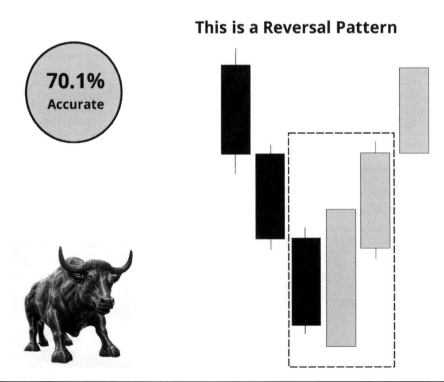

Bearish Belt Hold Candlestick Pattern

This pattern consists of a long bullish candle followed by a bearish candle that opens higher than the previous candles close, has a long body and a small or no lower wick.

This is a Reversal Pattern

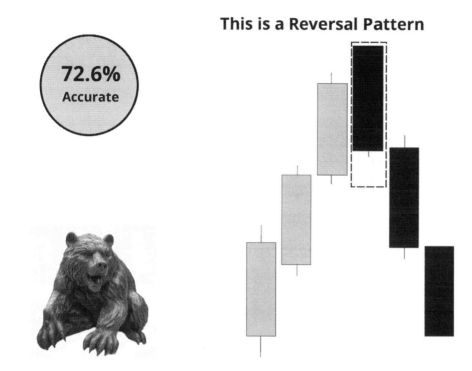

72.6% Accurate

Bullish Belt Hold Candlestick Pattern

This pattern consists of a long bearish candle followed by a bullish candle that opens lower than the previous candles close, has a long body and a small or no lower wick.

This is a Reversal Pattern

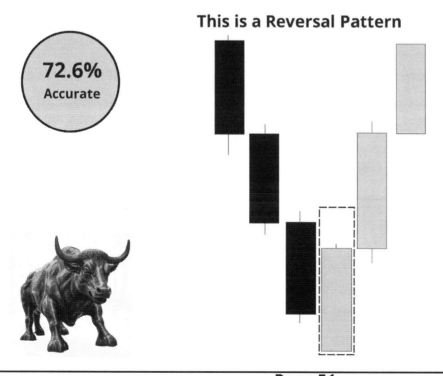

72.6% Accurate

Bullish Doji Star Candlestick Pattern

This a three candle pattern. The first candle is a long bearish candle at the bottom of a bearish trend. The second candle is a doji candle that opens and closes with a gap below the first candle. The third candle is a long bullish candle that closes above the midpoint of the first candle.

This is a Reversal Pattern

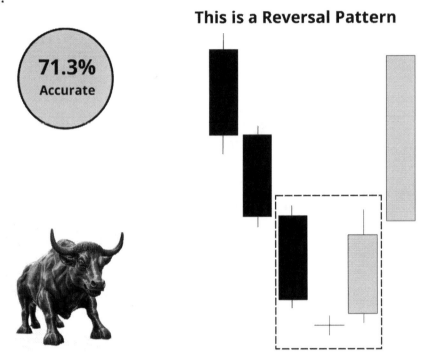

Bearish Doji Star Candlestick Pattern

This a three candle pattern. The first candle is a long bullish candle at the top of a bullish trend. The second candle is a doji candle that opens and closes with a gap above the first candle. The third candle is a long bearish candle that closes below the midpoint of the first candle.

This is a Reversal Pattern

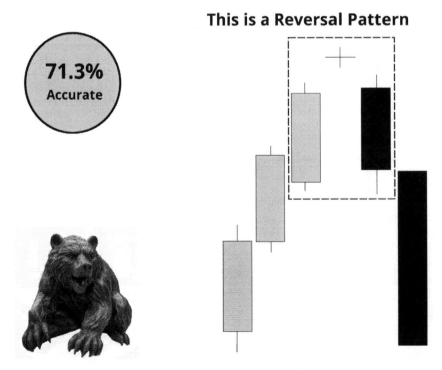

Homing Pigeon Candlestick Pattern

A two candlestick bullish pattern. The first candle is a long bearish candle at the bottom of a downtrend. The second candle is a bearish candle with an opening and closing price that fall inside the first candle's opening and closing price.

This is a Reversal Pattern

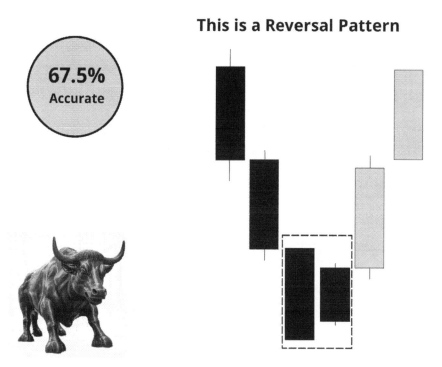

67.5% Accurate

Upside Gap Two Crows Candlestick Pattern

A three candlestick bullish pattern. The first candle is a long bullish candle that is part of an uptrend. The second candle is a bearish candle that gaps up and opens above the first candle. The third candle is a bearish candle that engulfs the 2nd candle, but closes above the first candle's closing price.

This is a Reversal Pattern

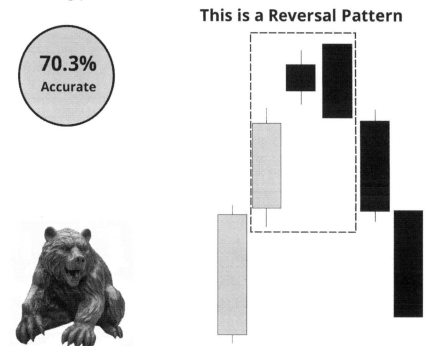

70.3% Accurate

Page 53

Bullish Piercing Line Candlestick Pattern

This two candle pattern starts with a bearish candle that is part of a downtrend. The second candle is bullish and opens below the close of the first candle and then closes above the midpoint of the first candle.

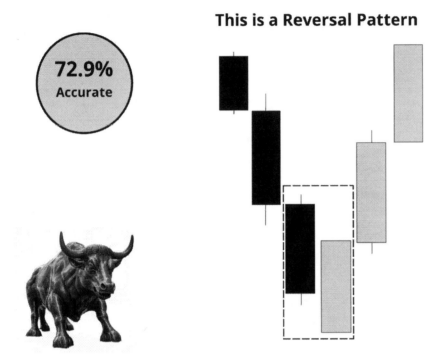

This is a Reversal Pattern

72.9% Accurate

Bearish Piercing Line Candlestick Pattern

This two candle pattern starts with a bullish candle that is part of an uptrend. The second candle is bearish and opens above the close of the first candle and then closes below the midpoint of the first candle.

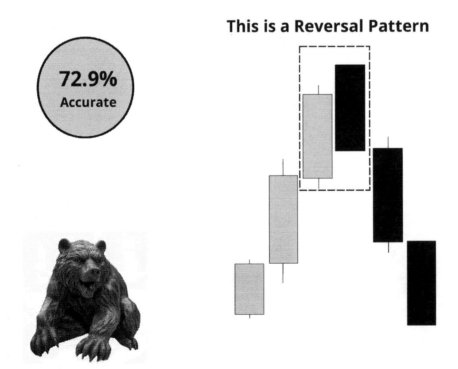

This is a Reversal Pattern

72.9% Accurate

Bullish Rickshaw Man Candlestick Pattern

A single doji candle characterized by having an open and close that are nearly the same price and sits in the center of a long upper and lower wick and occurs at the end of a downtrend.

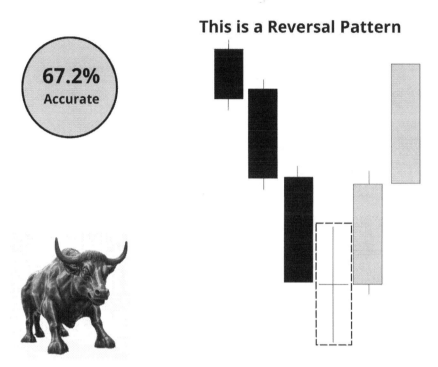

Bearish Rickshaw Man Candlestick Pattern

A single doji candle characterized by having an open and close that are nearly the same price and sits in the center of a long upper and lower wick and occurs at the end of an uptrend.

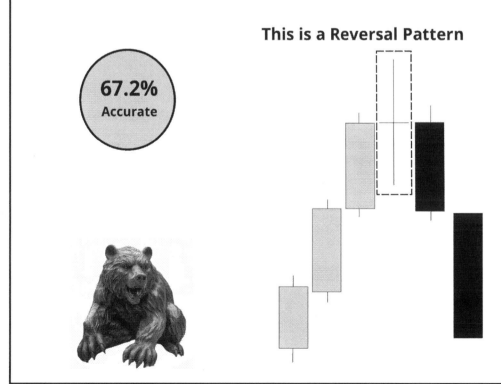

Bullish Spinning Top Candlestick Pattern

A bullish candle that appears at the bottom of a downtrend and characterized by a small body centered between long high and low wicks.

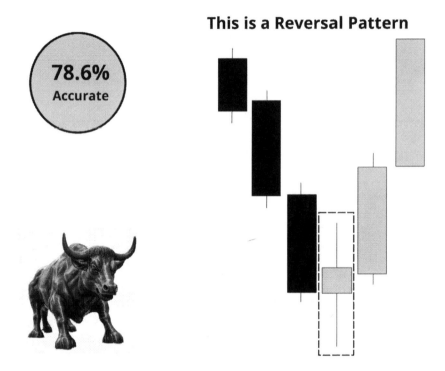

Bearish Spinning Top Candlestick Pattern

A bearish candle that appears at the bottom of a downtrend and characterized by a small body centered between long high and low wicks.

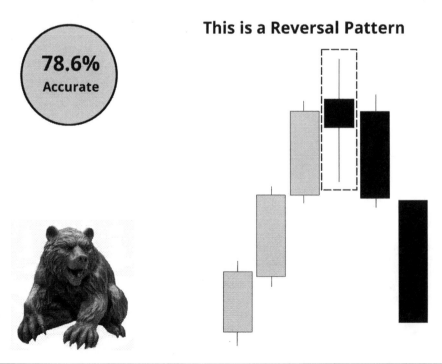

Takuri Candlestick Pattern

A candle with a small body, a long lower wick, and no upper wick. The candle is found at the bottom of a downtrend,

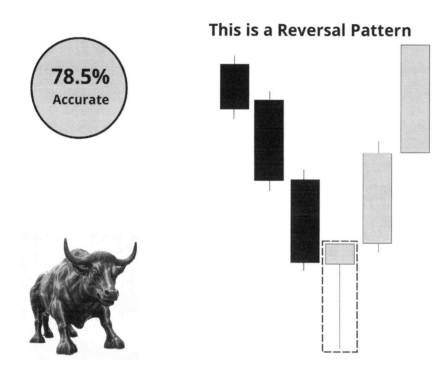

Two Crows Candlestick Pattern

A three candle pattern. The first candle is a long bullish candle at the top of an uptrend. The second candle is a bearish candle that gaps up from the first candle. The final candle is a long bearish candle that opens above the second candle and closes below the second candle, but closes above the first candle.

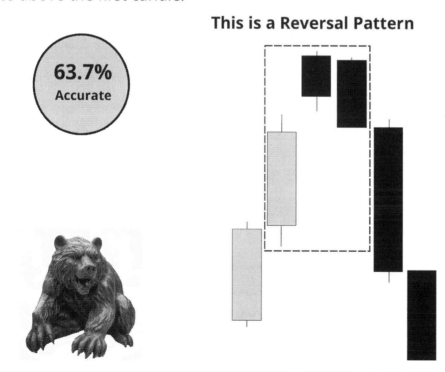

Identical Three Crows Candlestick Pattern

A three candle pattern that happens at the top of an uptrend. Consists of three bearish candles that have nearly the same range in price. Each consecutive candle opens near the close of the previous candle.

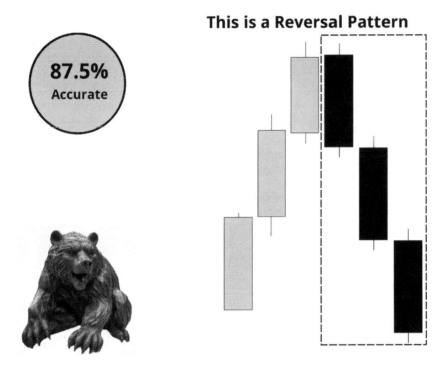

Matching Low Candlestick Pattern

A two candle pattern that occurs at the bottom of a downtrend. The two candles are bearish and close at or very near the same price level.

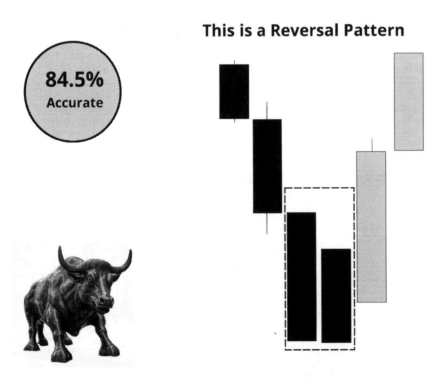

Bullish Tasuki Gap Candlestick Pattern

A three candlestick pattern. The first candle is a long bullish candle at the top of an uptrend followed by a second bullish candle that opens with a gap above the first candle. The final candle is a bearish candle that opens below the open of the second candle and partially closes the gap between the first and second candles.

This is a Continuation Pattern

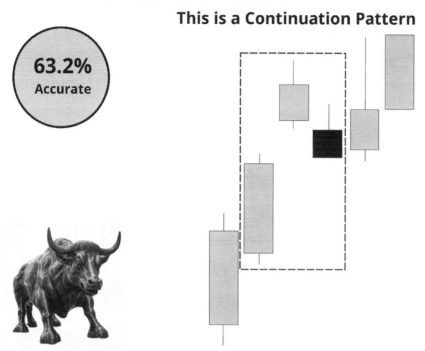

63.2% Accurate

Bearish Tasuki Gap Candlestick Pattern

A three candlestick pattern. The first candle is a long bearish candle at the bottom of a downtrend followed by a second bearish candle that opens with a gap below the first candle. The final candle is a bullish candle that opens above the open of the second candle and partially closes the gap between the first and second candles.

This is a Continuation Pattern

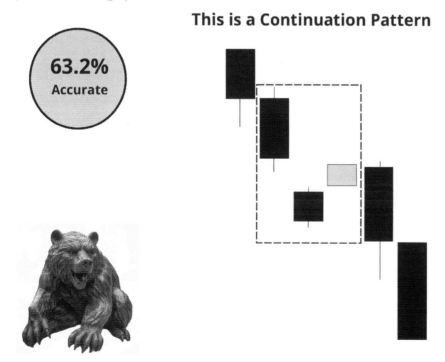

63.2% Accurate

Bullish Harami Cross Candlestick Pattern

A two candlestick pattern. The first candle is a long bearish candle at the end of a downtrend. The second candle is a doji candle that opens and closes within the price range of the body of the first candle.

This is a Reversal Pattern

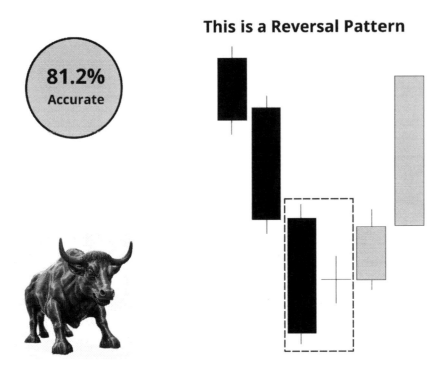

81.2% Accurate

Bearish Harami Cross Candlestick Pattern

A two candlestick pattern. The first candle is a long bullish candle at the end of an uptrend. The second candle is a doji candle that opens and closes within the price range of the body of the first candle.

This is a Reversal Pattern

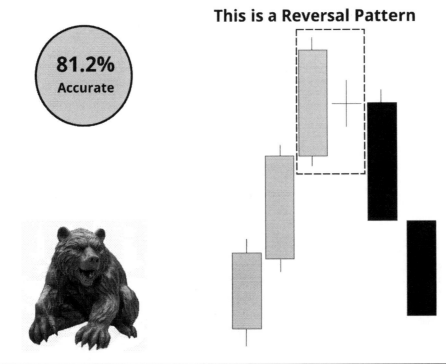

81.2% Accurate

Unique Three River Candlestick Pattern

A three candlestick pattern. The first candle is a long bearish candle at the end of a downtrend. The second candle is a hammer candle with a lower wick that makes a new low. The third candle is bullish and opens and closes within the high and low of the 2nd candle.

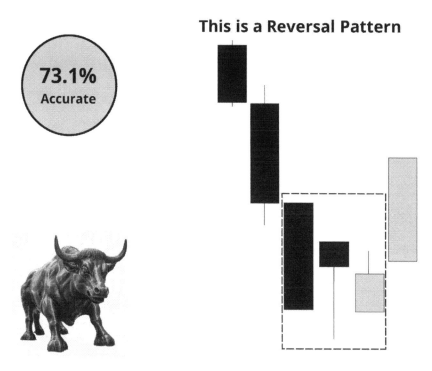

This is a Reversal Pattern

73.1% Accurate

Advance Block Candlestick Pattern

A three candlestick pattern. The first candle is a long bullish candle. The next candles are bullish and each a have smaller body and a longer wick than the previous candle.

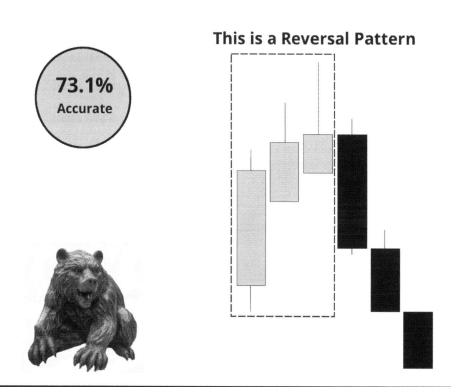

This is a Reversal Pattern

73.1% Accurate

CHAPTER 4

- **Quizzes: Try and Find the Hidden Patterns within the Charts**

Test Your Memory

The Following Quizzes Should Help you Identifiy Candlestick Patterns Within Larger Chart Time frames

Within the puzzles below are common candlestick patterns. You can mark your answers in pencil or make a mental note and check your solutions so that you can repeat the test to improve your accuracy until you're 100% successful. Give yourself bonus points if you correctly identify any patterns that are not in the answer pages in chapter 5.

Quiz #   In the chart below are a Bearish Tweezer, Bearish Harami, Bullish Harami, Bull Flag patterns, and a Hanging Man candle. Can you find them all?

Quiz 1 In the chart below are a Bearish Tweezer, Bearish Harami, Bullish Harami, Bull Flag patterns, and a Hanging Man candle. Can you find them all?

Quiz 2 In the chart below are a Bull Flag, Bear Flag, Morning Star, and Bearish Tweezer patterns. Can you find them all?

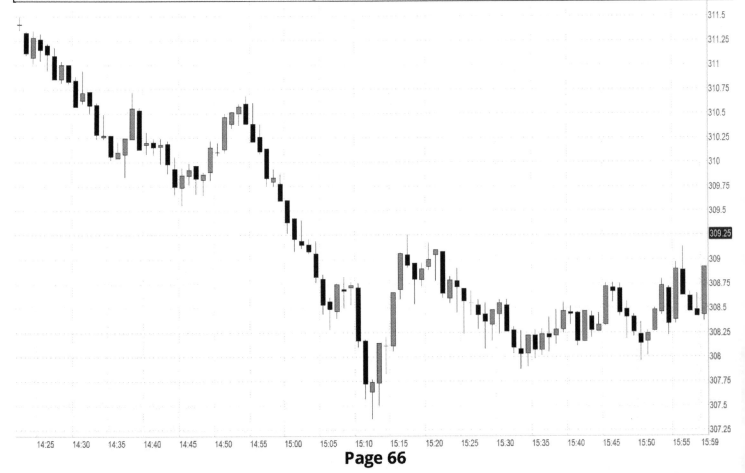

Quiz 3   In the chart below are 2 Bull Flags, a Bear Flag, Bullish Tweezer, Bearish Tweezer, and Bearish Harami candlestick patterns. Can you find them all?

Quiz 4   In the chart below are Three Black Crows (twice), 2 Bearish Tweezers patterns and a Hanging Man candle. Can you find them all?

Quiz 5 — In the chart below are 2 Bull Flag, Bullish Engulfing candlestick patterns, and a Dragonfly candle. Can you find them all?

Quiz 6 — In the chart below are 2 Bearish Tweezer, 2 Bullish Tweezer, and Morning Star patterns. Can you find them all?

Quiz 7 — In the chart below are 3 Bearish Tweezer, and 4 Bullish Tweezer patterns. Can you find them all?

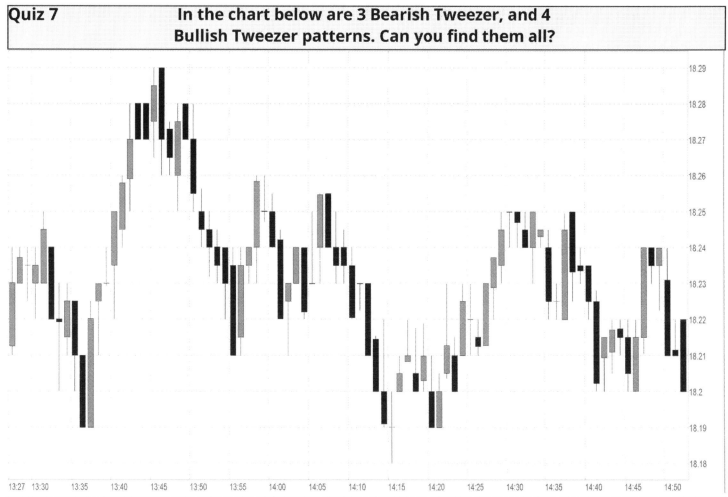

Quiz 8 — In the chart below are a Flat Top Break Out, 2 Bearish Tweezer, 3 Bullish Tweezer patterns, and a Hammer candle. Can you find them all?

Quiz 9 — In the chart below are 2 Bearish Tweezer, Bullish Tweezer, and Bear Flag patterns. Can you find them all?

Quiz 10 — In the chart below are 3 Bearish Tweezer, and Bull Flag patterns. Can you find them all?

Quiz 11 — In the chart below are a Bull Flag, 2 Flat Top Breakout, Bullish Tweezer patterns and a Shooting Star candle. Can you find them all?

Quiz 12 — In the chart below are a Bear Flag (with Three Black Crows), 2 Bearish Tweezer, Bullish Tweezer patterns and a Dragonfly candle. Can you find them all?

| Quiz 13 Answers | In the chart below are a Bull Flag, Bullish Tweezer, and Evening Star pattern. Can you find them all? |

| Quiz 14 | In the chart below are a Bullish Tweezer, 5 Bull Flag patterns and a Shooting Star candle. Can you find them all? |

Quiz 15 In the chart below are a Bear Flag, 2 Bearish Tweezer, Morning Star patterns and a Hammer candle, Can you find them all?

Quiz 16 In the chart below are a Bear Flag, Bull Flag, Bearish Tweezer patterns, a Hammer and Hanging Man candles. Can you find them all?

Quiz 17   **In the chart below are a Bull Flag, Bear Flag, Evening Star, Bullish Tweezer patterns. Can you find them all?**

Quiz 18   **In the chart below are a Bull Flag pattern, Hammer and Dragonfly candles. Can you find them all?**

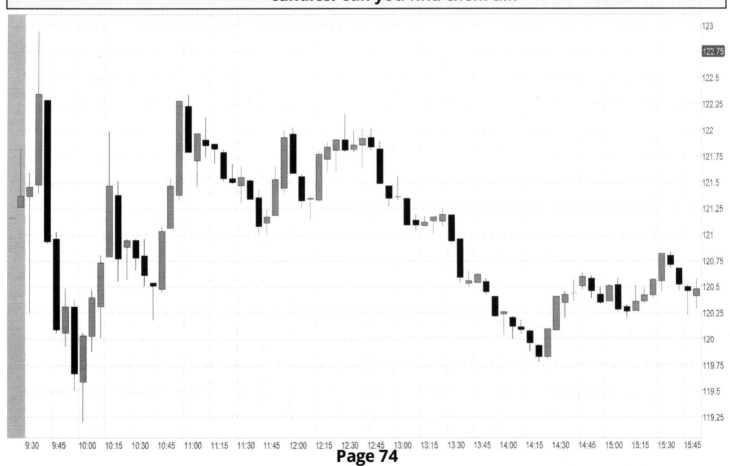

| Quiz 19 | In the chart below are 2 Bull Flags, 2 Bearish Tweezer patterns, a Dragonfly and 2 Hammer candles. Can you find them all? |

| Quiz 20 | In the chart below are Three White Soldiers, and 3 Bullish Tweezers patterns. Can you find them all? |

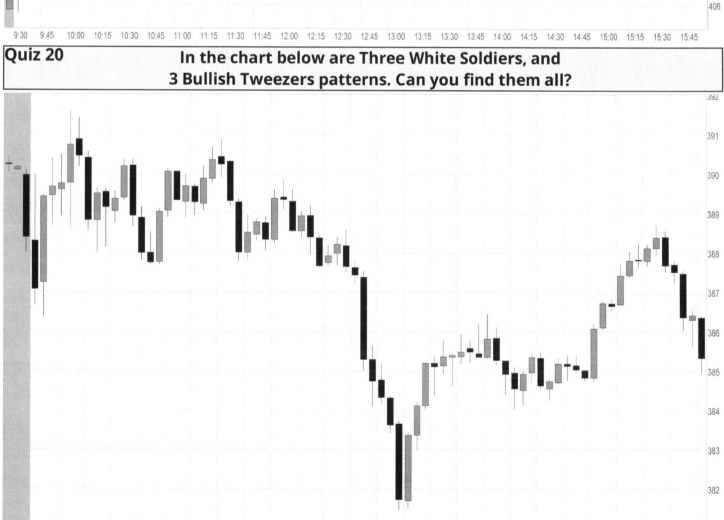

Quiz 21 — In the chart below are a Bearish Tweezer, Bullish Tweezer, Bearish Flag patterns and a Hammer candle. Can you find them all?

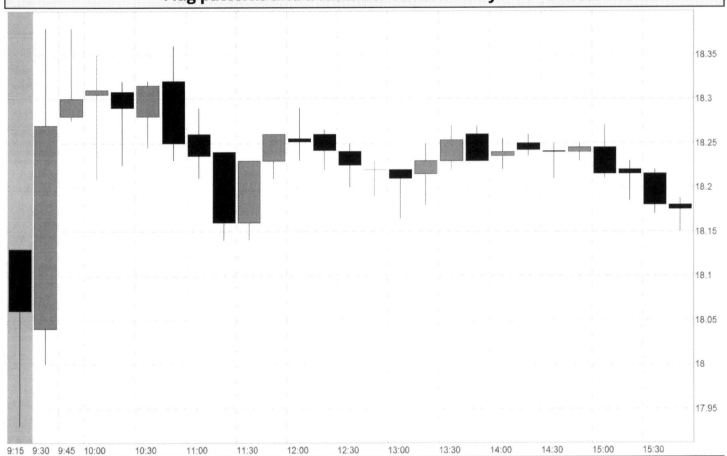

Quiz 22 — In the chart below are a Bearish Tweezer, Bullish Tweezer, Three Black Crow patterns and a Hammer candle. Can you find them all?

Quiz 23	In the chart below are a Shooting Star, Hammer, and Dragonfly candles. Can you find them all?

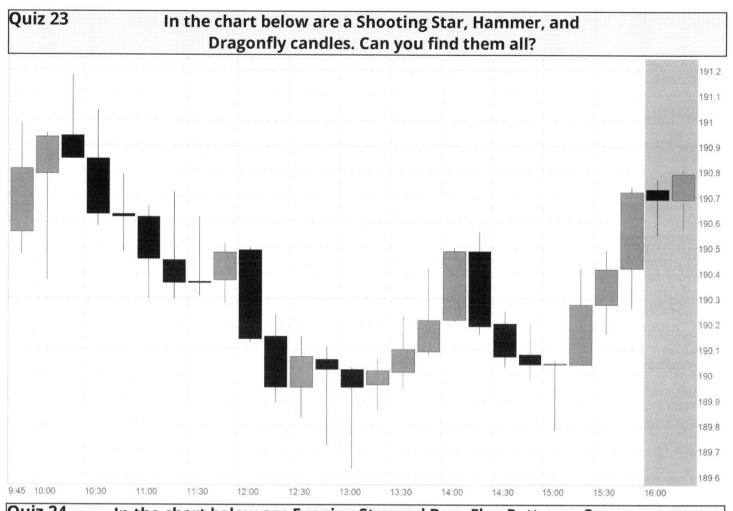

Quiz 24	In the chart below are Evening Star and Bear Flag Patterns. Can you find them both?

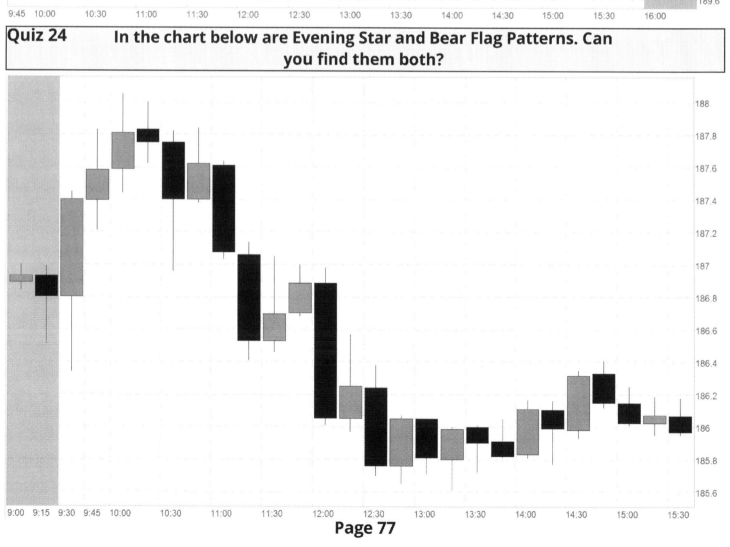

Quiz 25 — In the chart below are a Bearish Tweezer, Flat Top Breakout patterns and 2 Doji candles. Can you find them all?

Quiz 26 — In the chart below are a Bear Flag, 2 Bullish Tweezer patterns. Can you find them all?

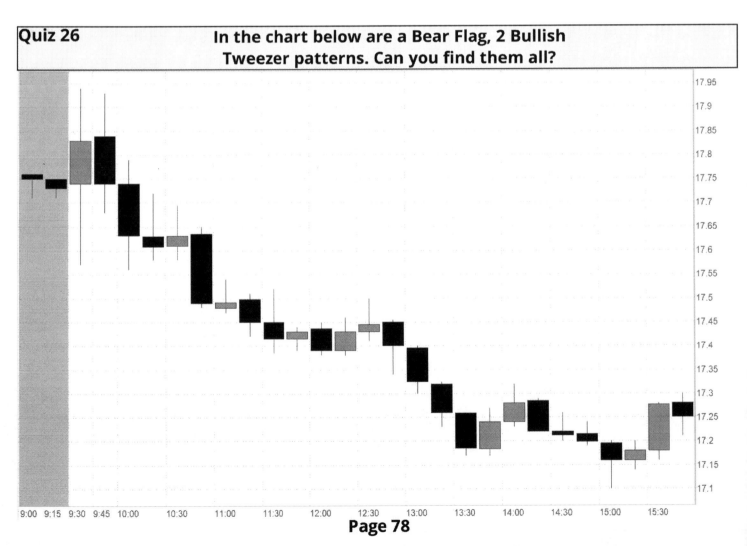

Quiz 27 — In the chart below are a Bullish Tweezer pattern, a Doji, 3 Hammer, and Inverted Hammer candles. Can you find them all?

Quiz 28 — In the chart below are a Bull Flag, Bullish Tweezer patterns, a Shooting Star, Dragon Fly, and Hammer candles. Can you find them all?

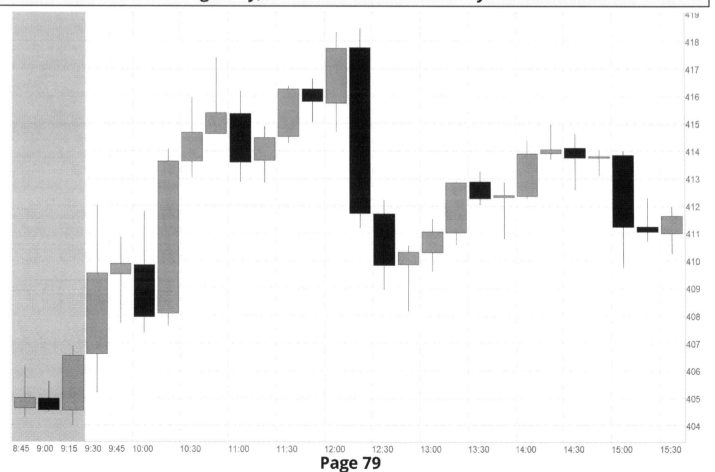

Quiz 29 — In the chart below are Bull Flag and Bearish Harami pattern. Can you find them both?

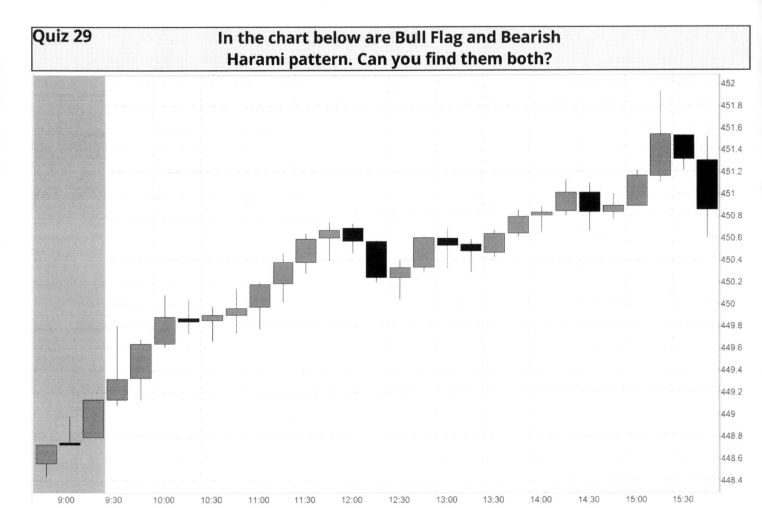

Quiz 30 — In the chart below are a Bull Flag, 2 Bearish Tweezer, and Evening Star patterns. Can you find them all?

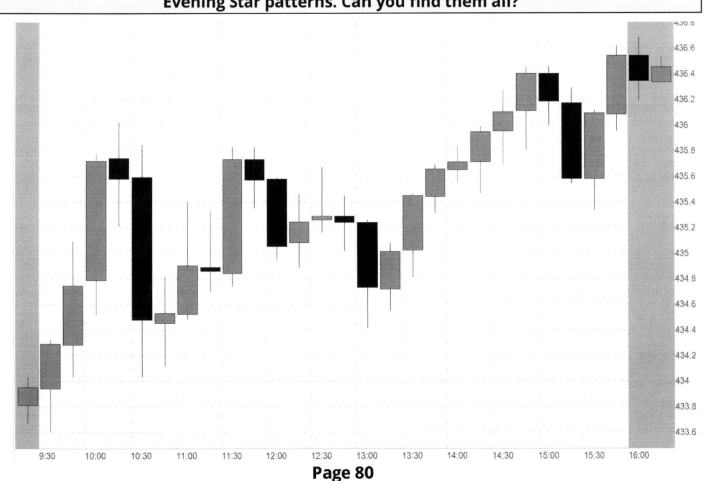

Quiz 31   In the chart below are 2 Bull Flag, Bearish Harami, and 1 Engulfing Candle patterns. Can you find them all?

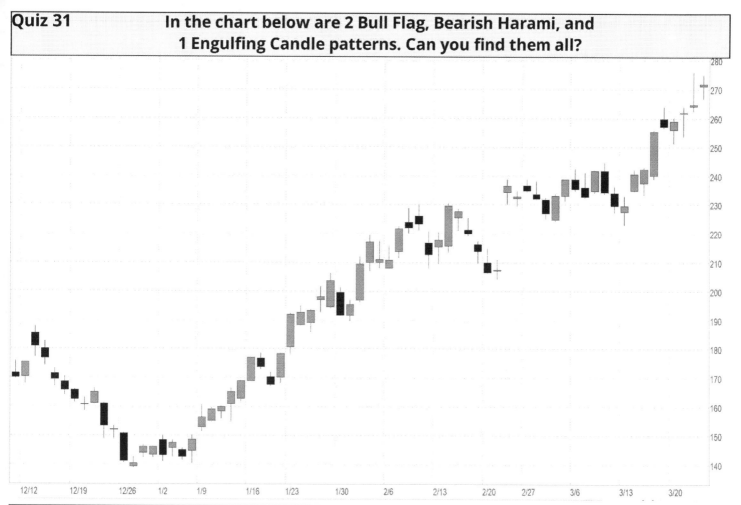

Quiz 32   In the chart below are a Flat Top Breakout and Evening Star patterns, a Gravestone and Inverted Hammer candles. Can you find them all?

Quiz 33	In the chart below are a Bull Flag and Morning Star patterns. Can you find them both?

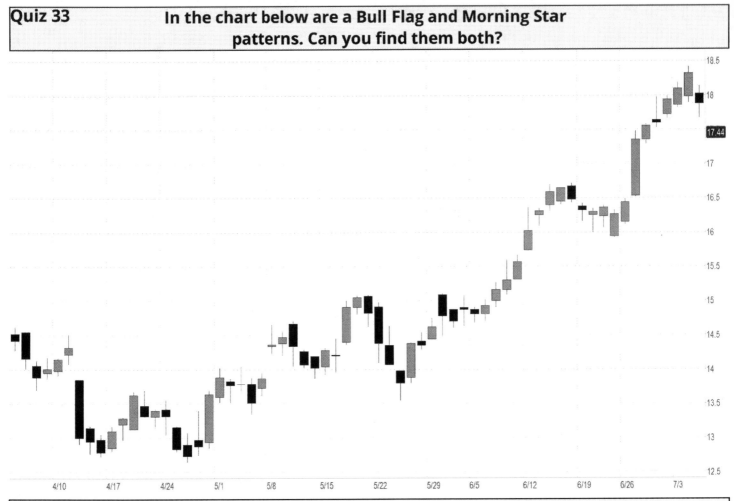

Quiz 34	In the chart below are a Bull Flag, 2 Engulfing Candle, Three White Soldiers, and 3 Bullish Tweezer patterns. Can you find them all?

Quiz 35 — In the chart below are a Bullish Tweezer, Bearish Tweezer, and Morning Star patterns. Can you find them all?

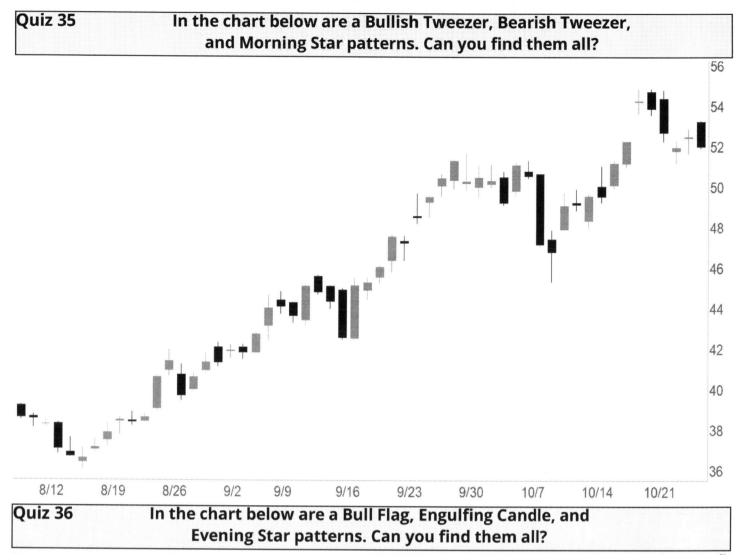

Quiz 36 — In the chart below are a Bull Flag, Engulfing Candle, and Evening Star patterns. Can you find them all?

Quiz 37 — In the chart below are 2 Bear Flag, 1 Bull Flag patterns, and a Hanging Man candle. Can you find them all?

Quiz 38 — In the chart below are Three Black Crows, Three White Soldiers, Bear Flag, and Bullish Harami patterns, and a Shooting Star candle. Can you find them all?

Quiz 39 — In the chart below are a Bullish Tweezer, Bullish Harami, and Flat Top Breakout patterns. Can you find them all?

Quiz 40 — In the chart below are a Bearish Tweezer, Bullish Tweezer, and Bull Flag patterns. Can you find them all?

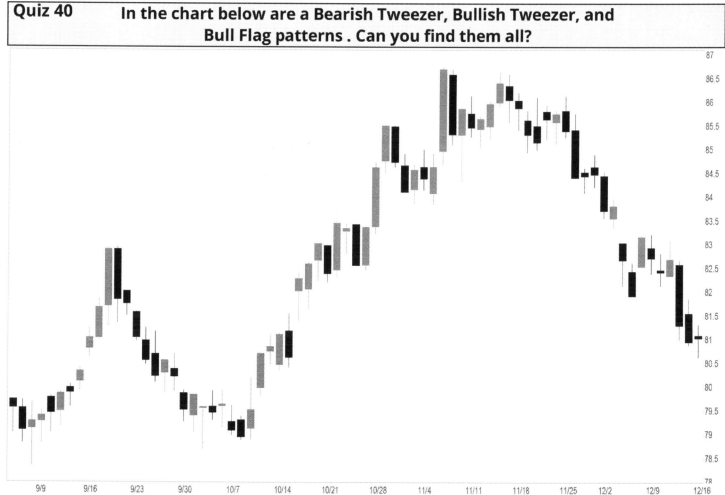

Quiz 41 In the chart below are a Cup & Handle, Bullish Abandoned Baby, Rising Three, Head and Shoulders, and Ladder Bottom patterns. Can you find them all?

Quiz 42 In the chart below are a Bullish Abandoned Baby, Falling Three, Ladder Top, Bearish Tweezer, and Bearish Harami patterns. Can you find them all?

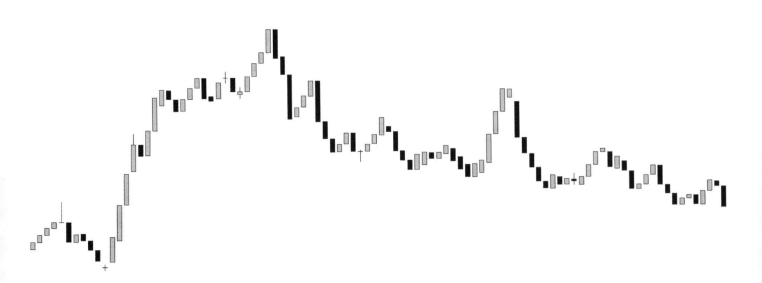

Quiz 43 In the chart below are a Bullish Mat Hold, Bearish Mat Hold, Dark Cloud Cover, Bullish Tweezer, and Flat Top Breakout patterns. Can you find them all?

Quiz 44 In the chart below are 2 Bearish Marubozu, 2 Bullish Marubozu candlesticks, and 3 Bull Flag patterns. Can you find them all?

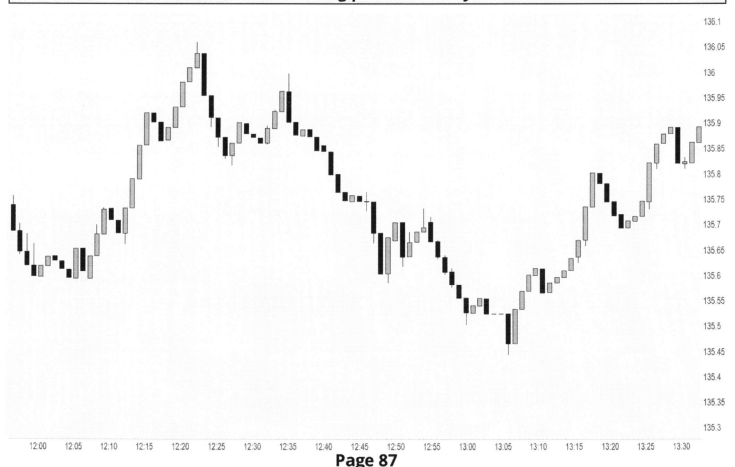

CHAPTER 5

- **Quiz Answers to the Hidden Patterns**

The Answers

The following pages contain the answers to the quizzes in Chapter 4. The answers are read by matching the numbered candlestick patterns to the numbered boxes that enclose the patterns. It is quite possible that other patterns may exist within the charts and we hope you will take the time to note them.

Good Luck!

How to Use the Answer Key

Quiz Number

Candlestick patterns numbered as they will be in the chart

Quiz # Answers: 1 Bull Flag, 2 Hanging Man, 3 Bearish Harami, 4 Bearish Tweezer, 5 Bullish Harami

The numbered boxes encompass the numbered candlestick patterns above

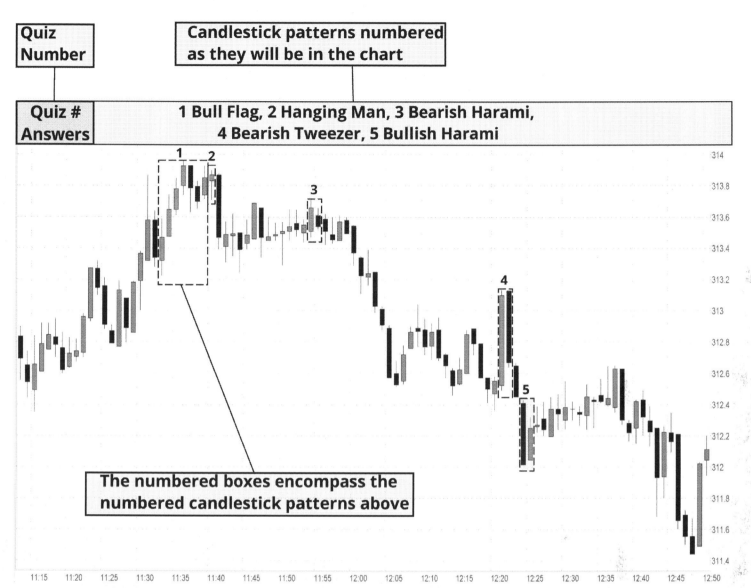

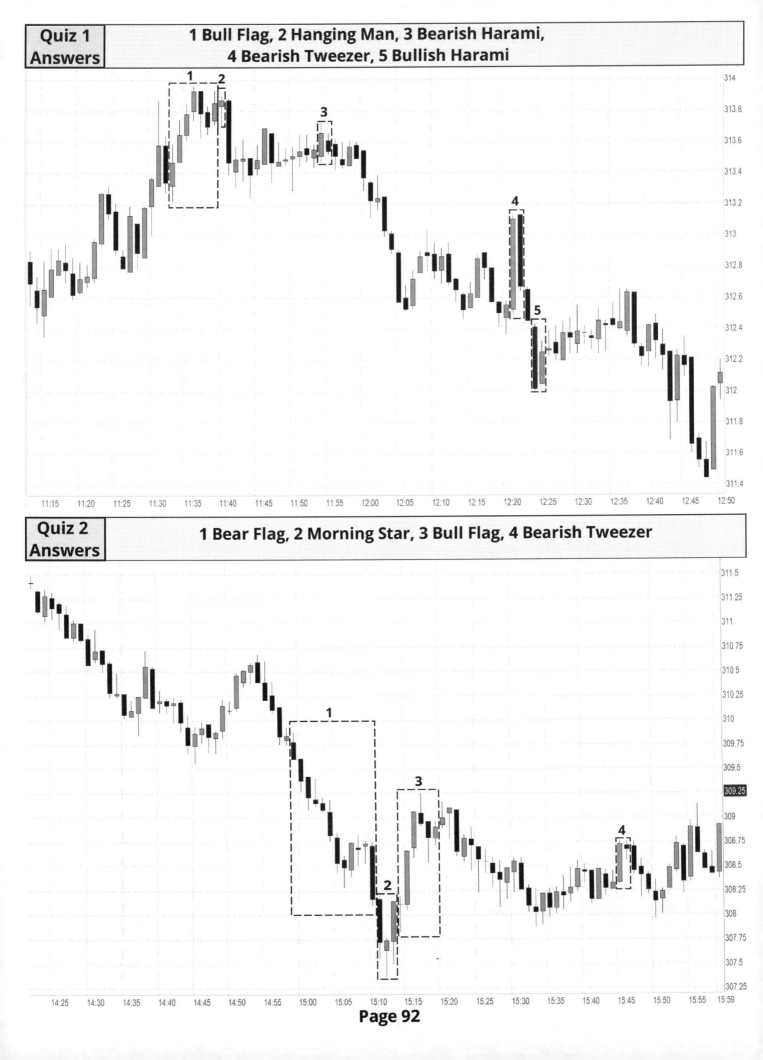

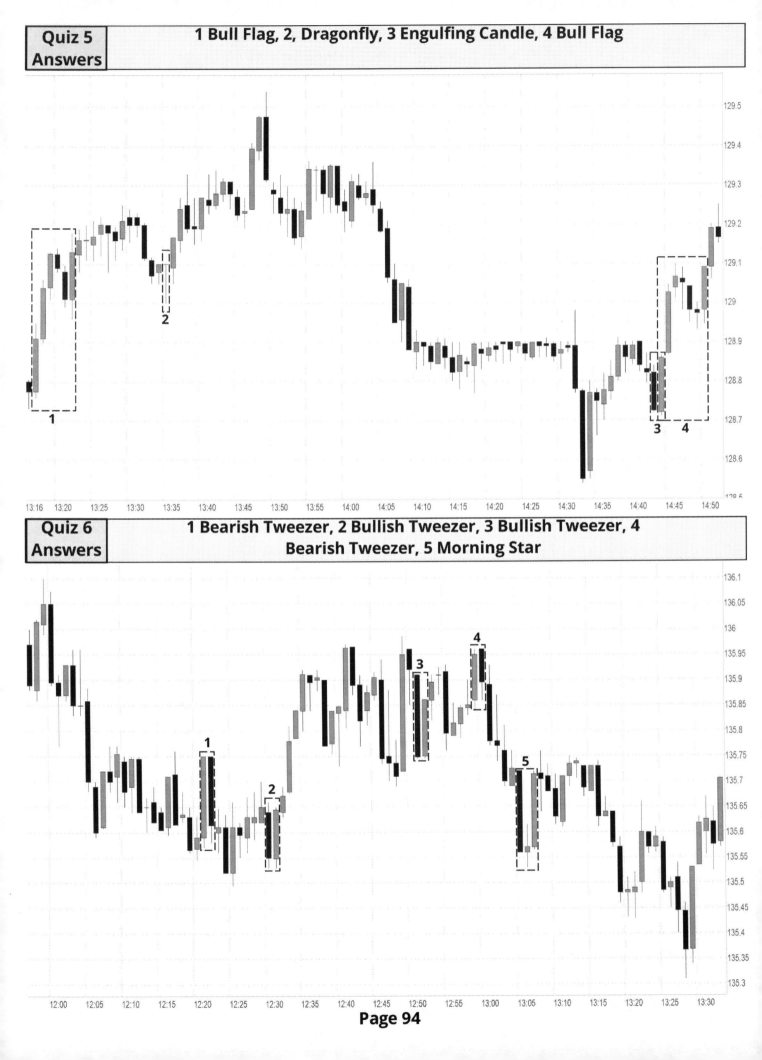

Quiz 7 Answers	1 Bullish Tweezer, 2 Bearish Tweezer, 3 Bullish Tweezer, 4 Bearish Tweezer, 5 Bullish Tweezer, 6 Bearish Tweezer, 7 Bullish Tweezer

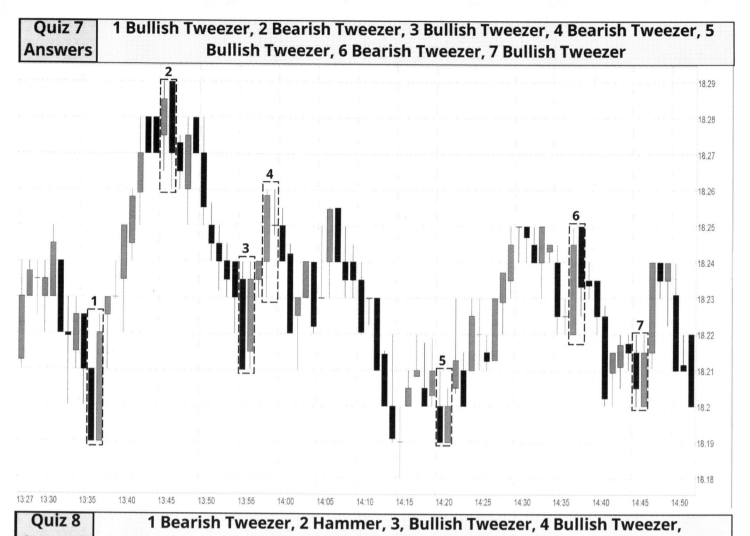

Quiz 8 Answers	1 Bearish Tweezer, 2 Hammer, 3, Bullish Tweezer, 4 Bullish Tweezer, 5 Flat Top Break Out, 6 Bearish Tweezer

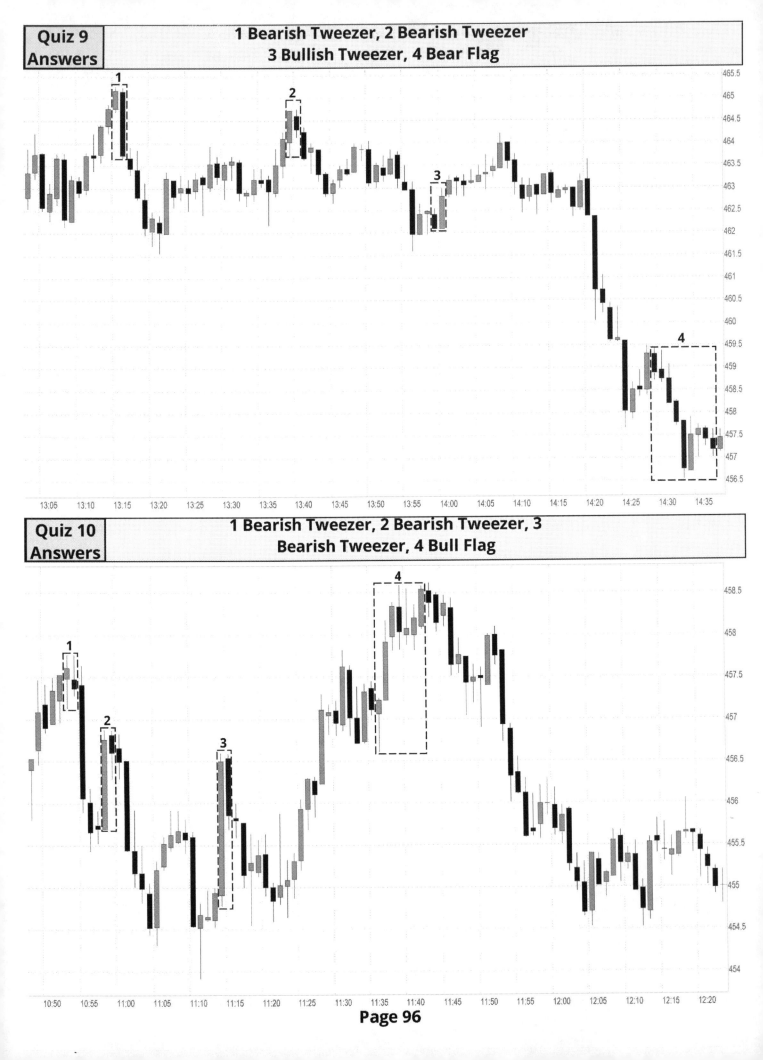

| Quiz 13 Answers | 1 Bullish Tweezer, 2 Bull Flag, 3 Evening Star. |

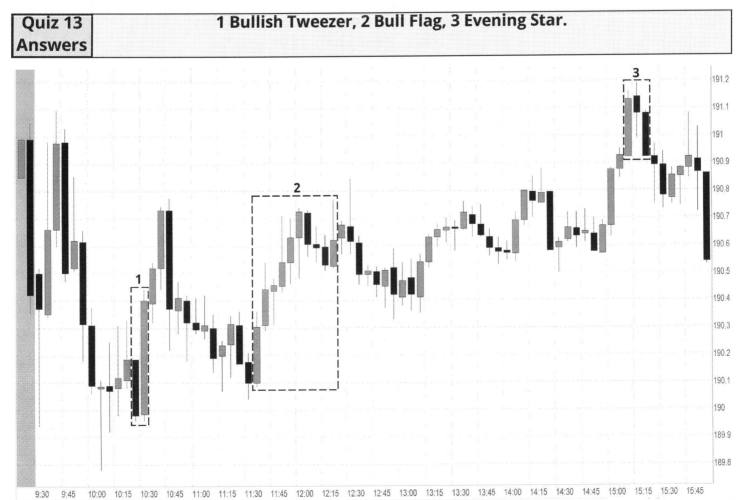

| Quiz 14 Answers | 1 Bullish Tweezer, 2 Bull Flag, 3 Bull Flag, 4, Bull Flag, 5 Bull Flag, 6 Bull Flag, 7 Shooting Star |

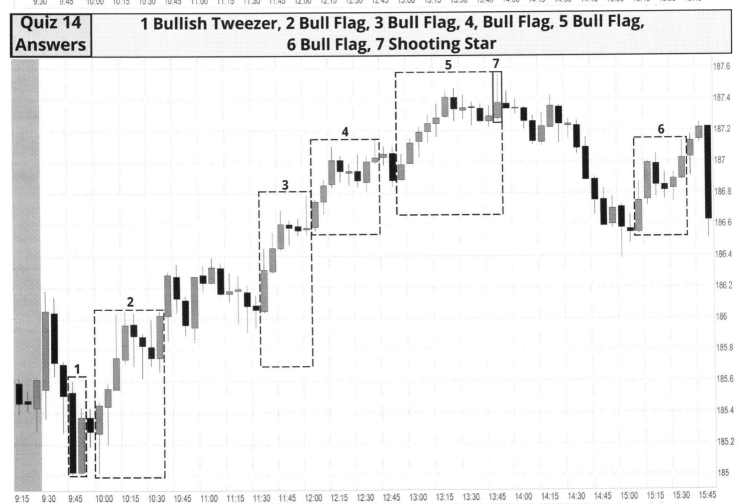

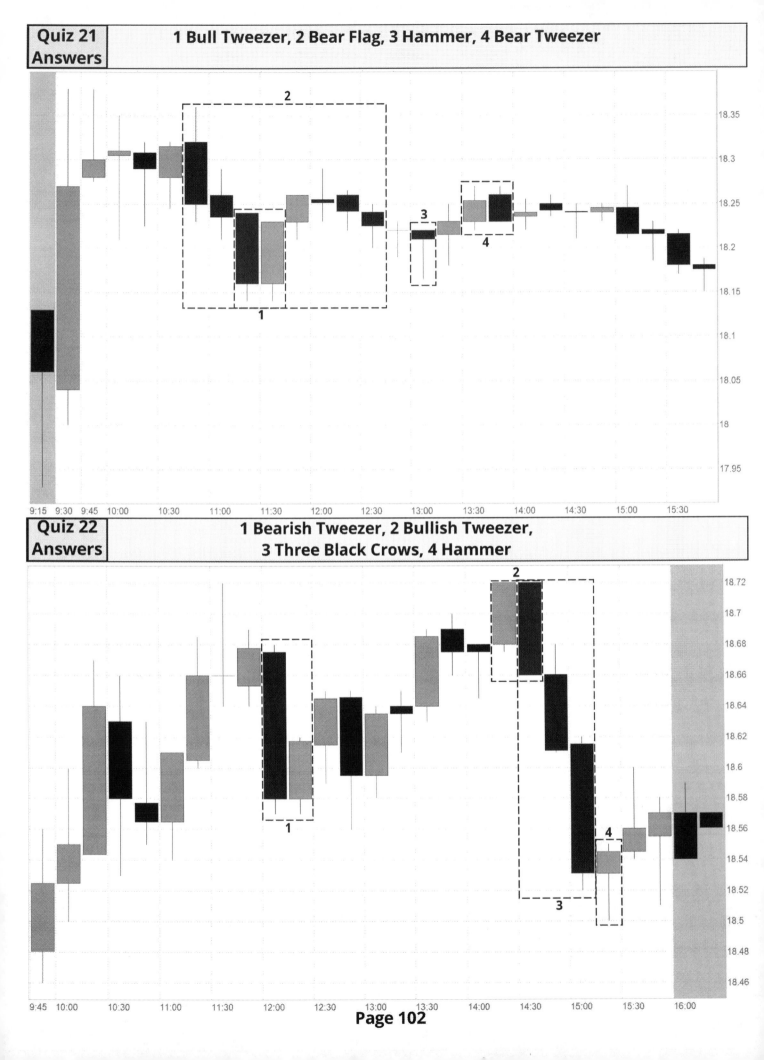

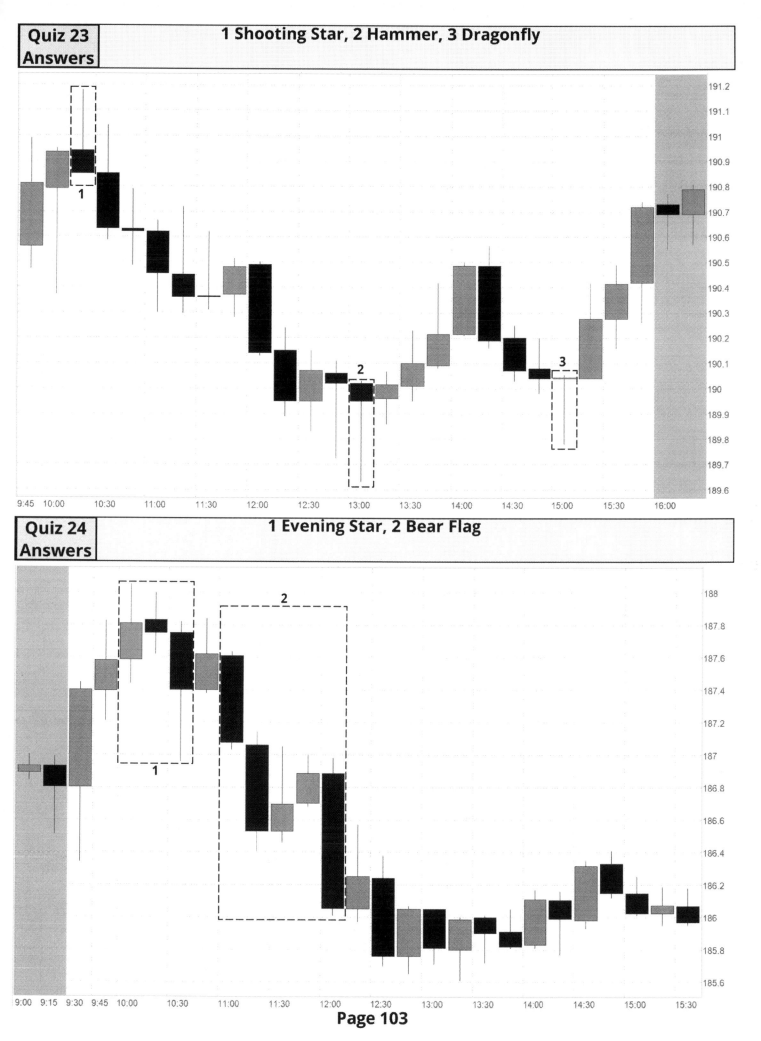

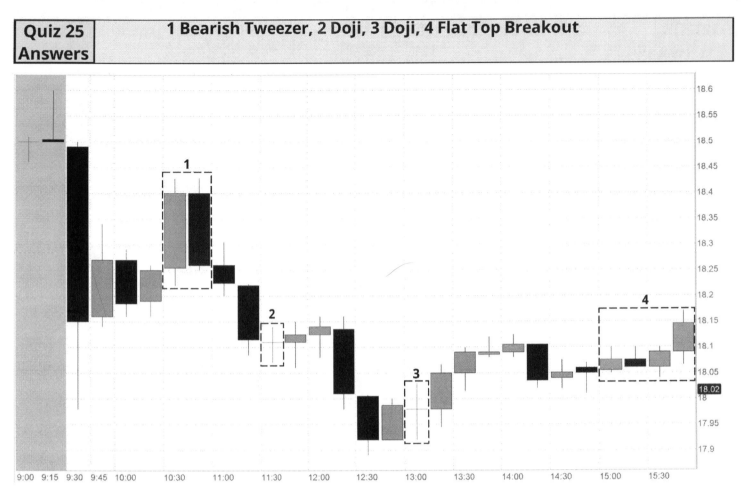

Quiz 25 Answers — 1 Bearish Tweezer, 2 Doji, 3 Doji, 4 Flat Top Breakout

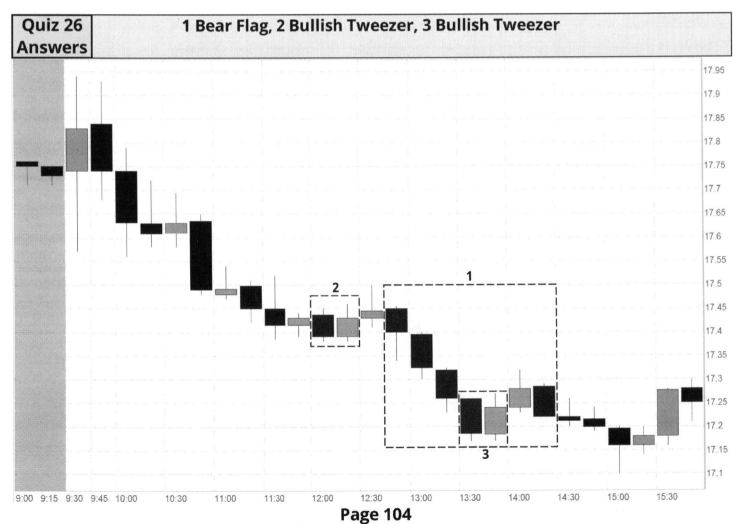

Quiz 26 Answers — 1 Bear Flag, 2 Bullish Tweezer, 3 Bullish Tweezer

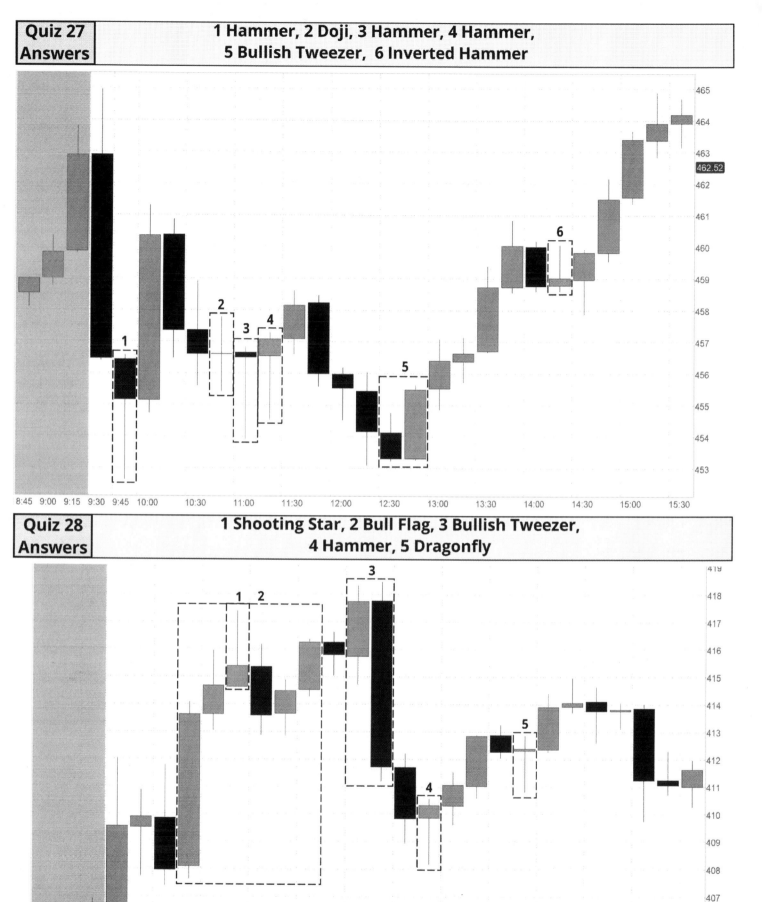

Quiz 29 Answers — 1 Bull Flag, 2 Bearish Harami

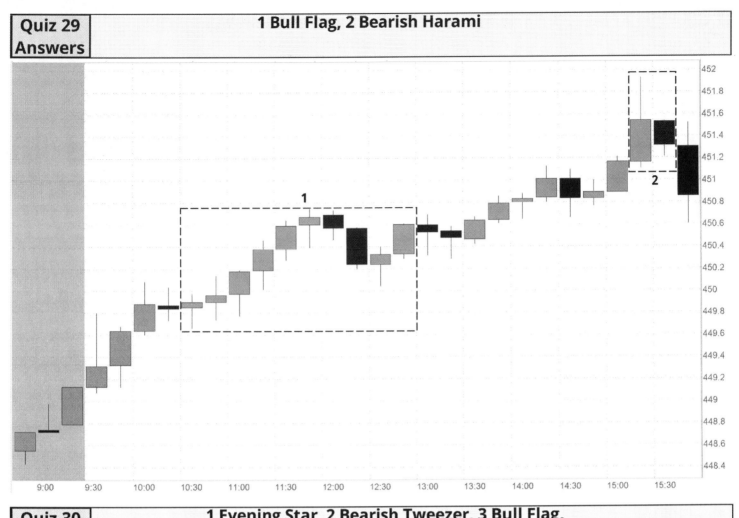

Quiz 30 Answers — 1 Evening Star, 2 Bearish Tweezer, 3 Bull Flag, 4 Bearish Tweezer

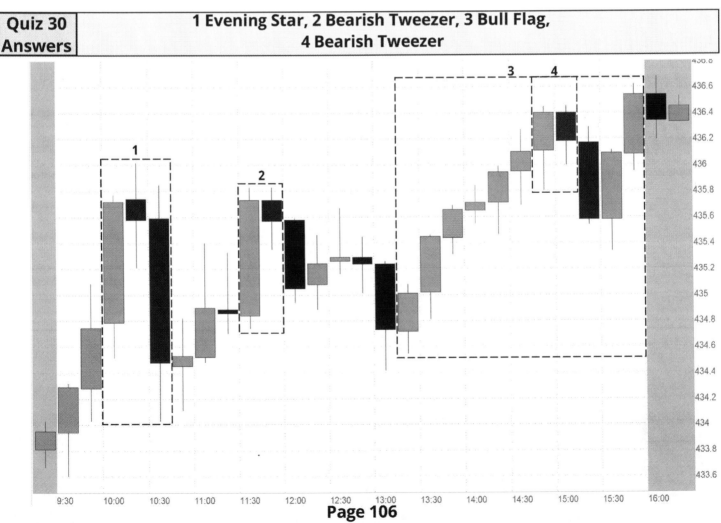

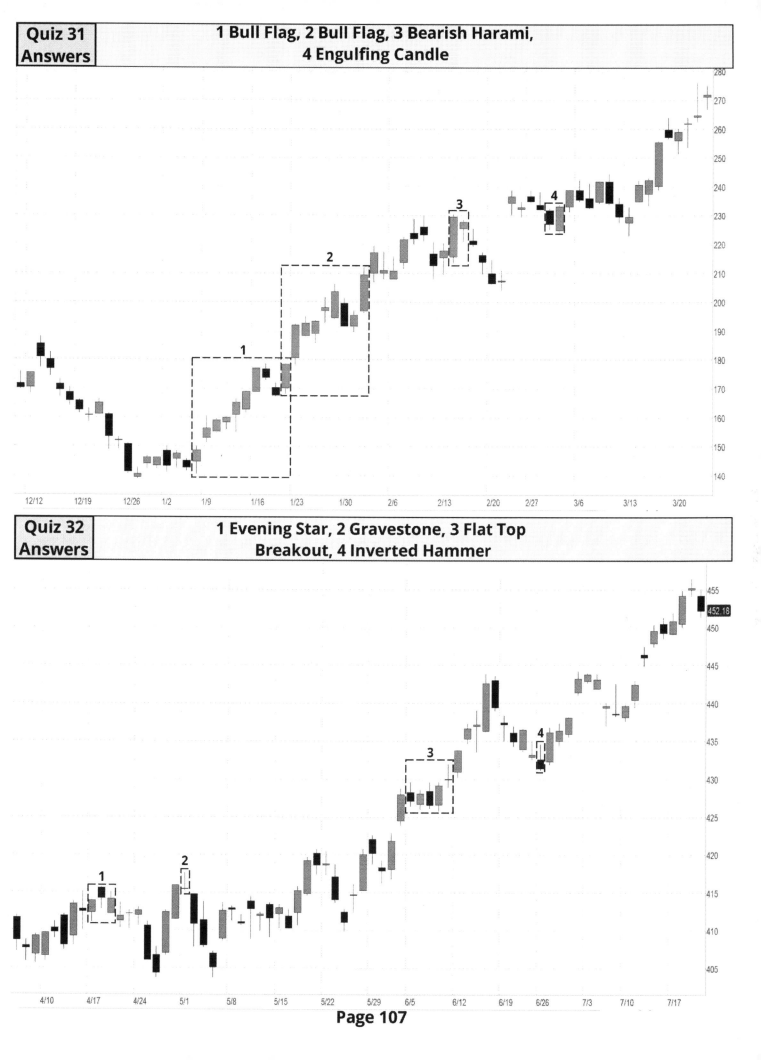

| Quiz 33 Answers | 1 Morning Star, 2 Bull Flag |

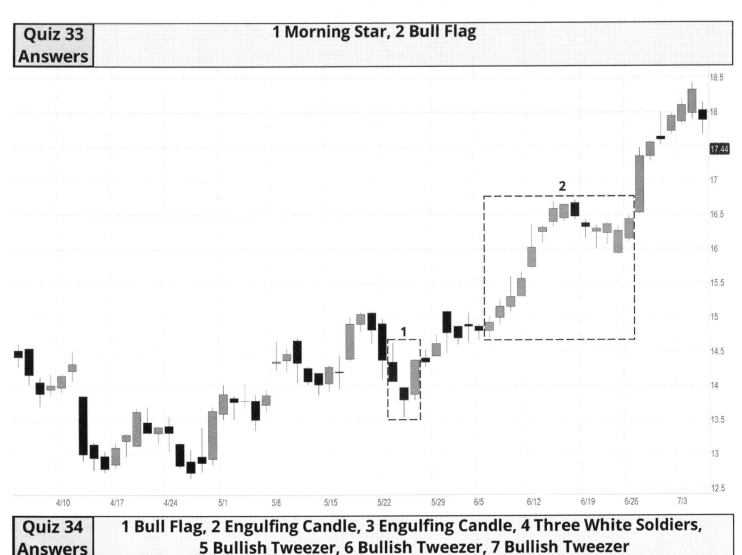

| Quiz 34 Answers | 1 Bull Flag, 2 Engulfing Candle, 3 Engulfing Candle, 4 Three White Soldiers, 5 Bullish Tweezer, 6 Bullish Tweezer, 7 Bullish Tweezer |

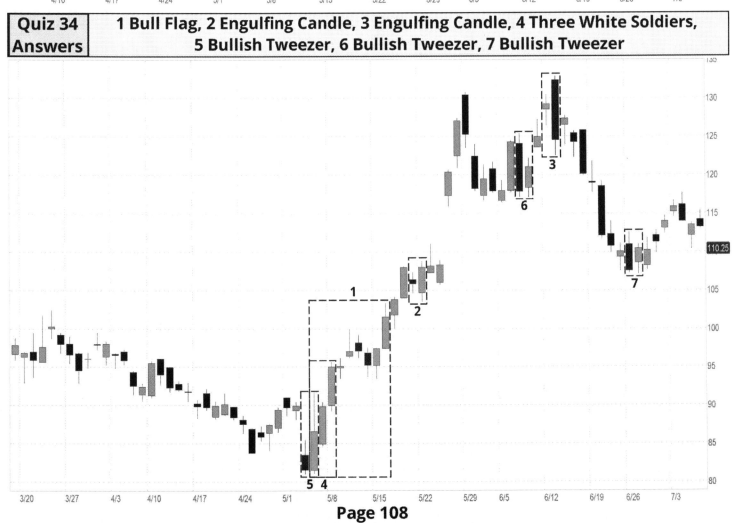

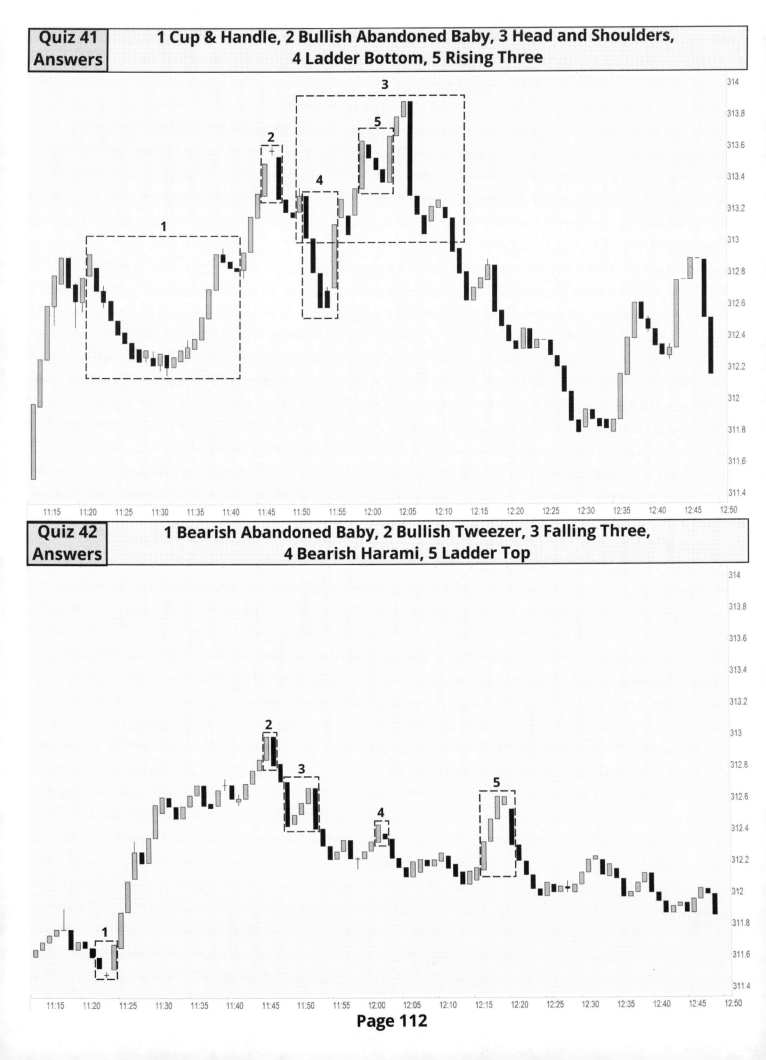

Quiz 43 Answers — 1 Bullish Tweezer, 2 Dark Cloud Cover, 3 Bearish Mat Hold, 4 Bull Mat Hold, 5 Flat Top Breakout

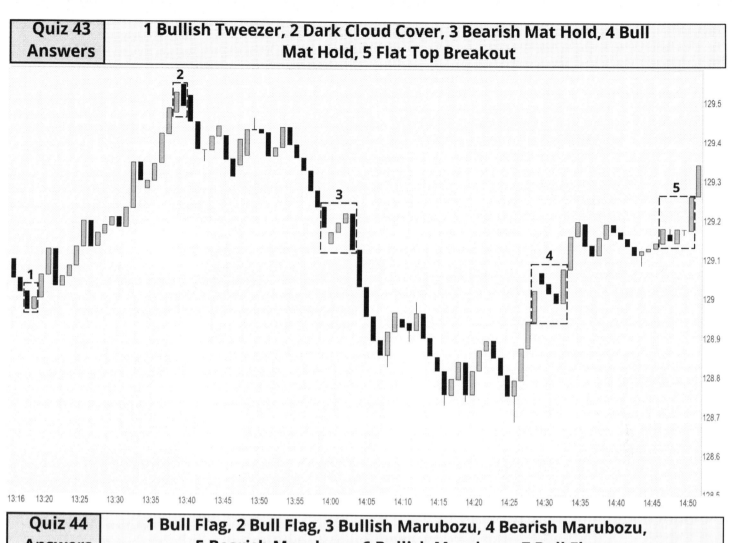

Quiz 44 Answers — 1 Bull Flag, 2 Bull Flag, 3 Bullish Marubozu, 4 Bearish Marubozu, 5 Bearish Marubozu, 6 Bullish Marubozu, 7 Bull Flag

Glossary of Common Trading Terms

- **Average Directional Index (ADX) -** measures the strength of a trend, regardless of its direction, using price movements
- **Average True Range (ATR)** - measures volatility and range of price movement over a given period
- **Bar Chart -** represents price movements, where each bar (candle) denotes a specific time frame
- **Bear Market -** market condition where prices are falling or expected to fall
- **Bollinger Bands -** measures volatility and range relative to its moving average
- **Breakout -** When a security's price moves outside a predefined support or resistance level
- **Breakout Volume** - the volume of trades during a price breakout, confirms the breakout's strength
- **Bull Market -** market condition where prices are rising or expected to rise
- **Candlestick Chart -** displays the high, low, opening, and closing price of a security for a specific period
- **Chart Patterns -** graphical formation created to identify price movement on a chart
- **Closing Price -** the final price a security is traded for in a given period or on a given day
- **Consolidation -** a period where prices move within a narrow range, indicating stability or indecision
- **Convergence and Divergence** - the movement of two or more indicators in relation to each other, used to predict future price movements
- **EMA - Exponential Moving Average** - tracks trend & support/resistance giving weight to more recent data
- **Fibonacci Retracements** - used to identify potential reversal levels on candlestick charts
- **Gap -** a break between prices on a chart when security takes a sharp move up or down with no trading in between
- **Heikin-Ashi Technique** - modifies candles to reduce noise and clarify trend direction
- **High -** the highest price at which a security is traded during a specific period
- **Keltner Channel** - volatility-based envelope set above and below an exponential moving average, similar to bollinger bands
- **Low -** The lowest price at which a security is traded during a specific period
- **Moving Average Convergence Divergence (MACD) -** a trend-following momentum indicator
- **Momentum Indicators -** track the speed of price changes in a security to identify trend strength
- **Open Price -** the starting price a security is traded for in a given period or on a given day
- **Oscillators -** indicators that vary within a band or range, typically identify overbought or oversold conditions
- **Pivot Points -** tracks support/resistance levels often showing a reversal of a current trend
- **Price Action -** movement of a security's price plotted over time
- **Relative Strength Index (RSI) -** tracks overbought/oversold conditions and momentum
- **Resistance Levels -** price level where selling pressure can overcome buying, halting rising prices
- **Stochastic Oscillator** - compares a security's closing price to its price range over a specific time, measuring momentum
- **Support Levels -** a price level where buying pressure can overcome selling, halting falling prices
- **Symbol** - a unique identifier assigned to a security for trading purposes
- **Technical Analysis -** the study of past market data to forecast future price movements
- **Time Frame -** the duration for which a trading chart illustrates the price movements of a security
- **Trend** - the general direction in which a security's price is moving over a period of time
- **Trend Line -** a straight line that connects a series of price points and extends into the future to act as a line of support or resistance
- **Volume** - tracks the number of shares or contracts being traded within a specific time period
- **Volume Profile -** tracks the volume traded at different price levels within a specific time period
- **VWAP -** Volume Weighted Average Price - calculating a price over a specific time period and is commonly used by institutional investors and day traders to assess the value of an asset and make trading decisions.

If You Liked the Book Don't Forget to Support the Author

Thank You!

CHAPTER 6

• Have fun as You Learn Your Candlestick Patterns with These Helpful Flashcards

Reading the Flashcards

FRONT

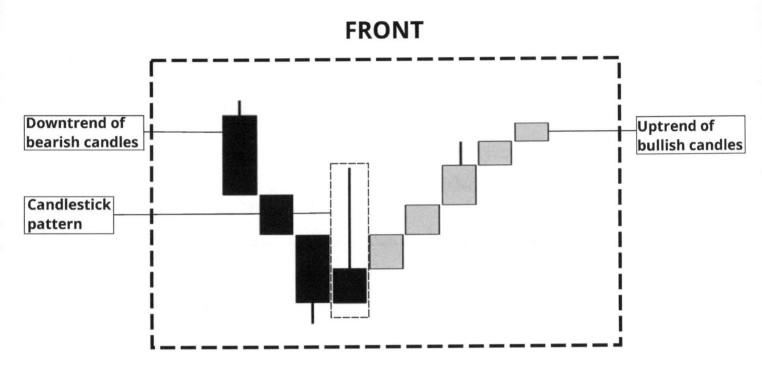

BACK

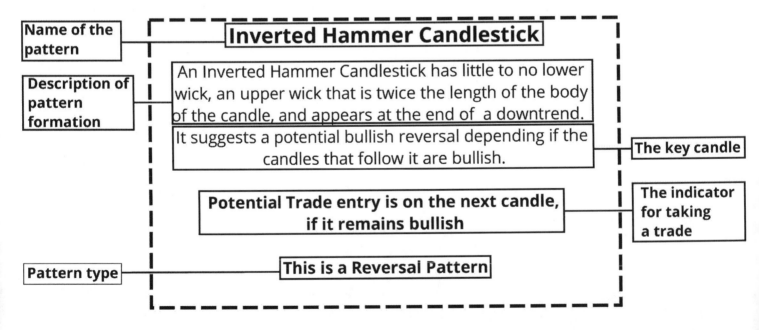

How to use your Flashcards in Chapter 6

The following flashcards are designed to be cut out of the book along the scissor lines. Then evenly cut each card out of the detached page to make 3 cards. If possible, it's a good idea to go to your local copy store or printer and laminate the individual cards or laminate the whole sheet that you detached and then cut the cards into 3 individual cards. The answers should line up on the back of each pattern creating a card you can carry anywhere to help test yourself or work with others and make a game out of it. You should end up with 65 different flash cards of the most commonly identified candlestick patterns used by day traders, scalpers. and swing traders

Tip: Try practicing with your trading friends to help learn

Start Cutting on the Next Page

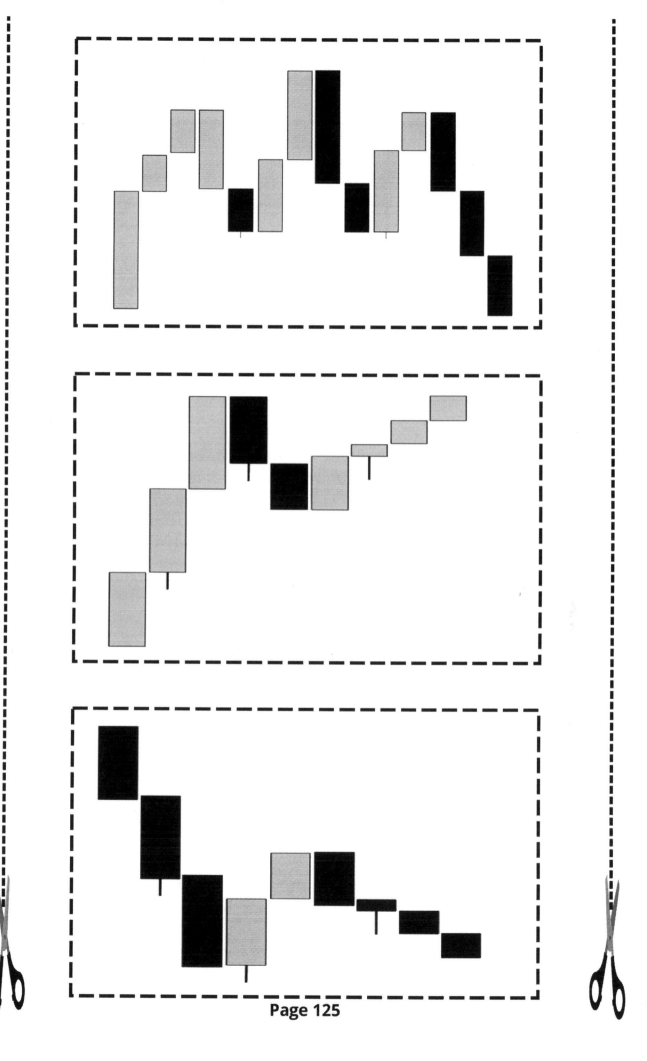

Head & Shoulders Pattern

A bearish pattern created by three peaks, a high center peak (the head) and a lower peak on each side (the shoulders). **The lowest candles on the troughs between the peaks** form a **support level** (the neck).
Potential trade entry is the next candle to break the support level

This is a Reversal Pattern

Bull Flag Pattern

A bullish pattern identified as a trend upwards (the pole), followed by a retracement (the flag - 2 or more candles with lower highs and lower lows) a **resistance level** is formed by **connecting the highs** of the retracement.
Potential Trade entry is the next candle to break the resistance level

This is a Continuation Pattern

Bear Flag Pattern

A bearish pattern recognized as a trend downwards (the pole), followed by a retracement (2 or more candles with higher highs and higher lows) a **support level** is formed by **connecting the lows** of the retracement.

Potential trade entry is the next candle to break the support level

This is a Continuation Pattern

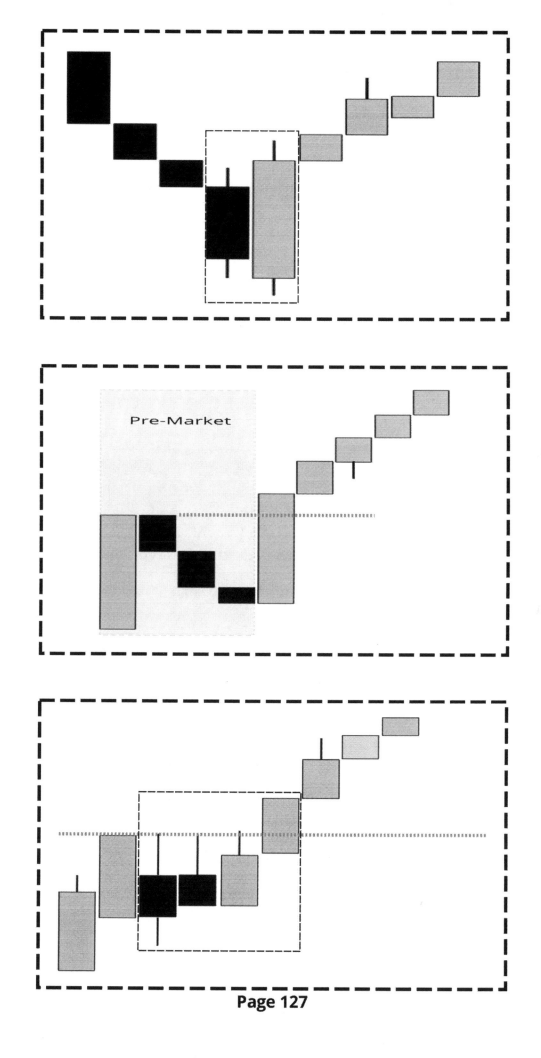

Bullish Engulfing Candlestick Pattern

A two candle bullish pattern characterized by a bearish candle followed by a bullish candle. The bearish candle is between the open and close of the bullish candle. The **high of the bullish candle** creates a **resistance level**. Potential trade entry is the next candle, if it breaks the resistance level.

This is a Reversal Pattern

Breakout of Premarket High Pattern

A bullish Pattern that identifies the highest price of premarket and waits for the first candle in open session market to break that level. The **premarket high** acts as a **resistance level**. Potential trade entry is the first candle to break the resistance level.

This is a Breakout Pattern

Flat-top Breakout Pattern

A bullish Pattern that forms as multiple bullish candles reach the same price level. The high of these candles acts as a resistance level. Potential trade entry is the first candle to break the resistance level.

This is a Breakout Pattern

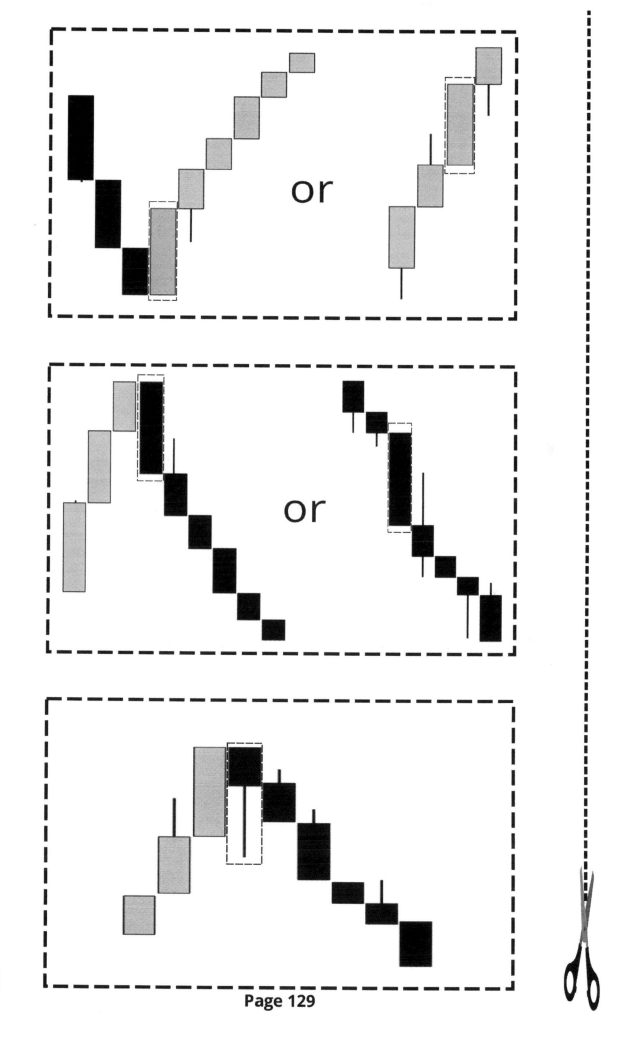

Bullish Marubozu Candlestick

A Bullish Marubozu is a long body with no or minimal shadows that closes higher than it opens, indicating a strong bullish sentiment. Depending on where it appears in a trend it can be an indicator of support for the reversal of a downtrend or the continuation of an uptrend.

Potential trade entry is on the next candle, if it remains bullish

This is a Reversal or Continuation Pattern

Bearish Marubozu Candlestick

A Bearish Marubozu is a long body with no or minimal shadows that closes lower than it opens, indicating a strong bearish sentiment. Depending on where it appears in a trend it can be an indicator of support for a reversal of an uptrend or continuation of a downtrend.

Potential trade entry is on the next candle, if it remains bearish

This is a Reversal or Continuation Pattern

Hanging Man Candlestick

A Hanging Man Candlestick is identified by a lower wick that is at least twice the length of the body of the candle, little to no upper wick, and appearing after an uptrend. It suggests a potential bearish reversal if confirmed by subsequent price action.

Potential trade entry is on the next candle, if it remains bearish

This is a Reversal Pattern

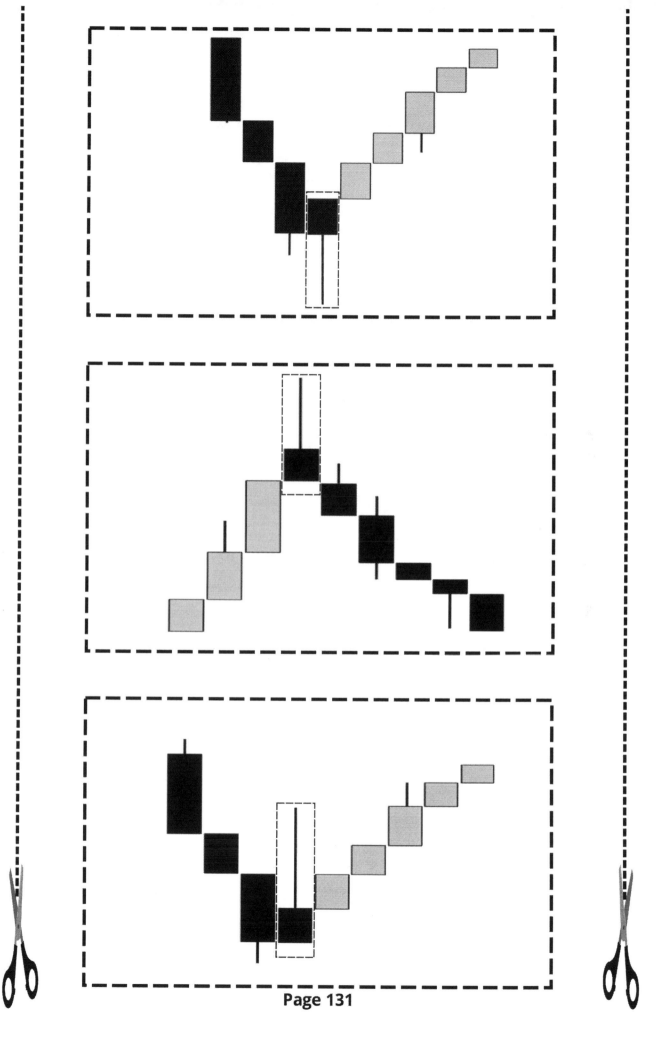

Hammer Candlestick

A Hammer Candlestick is noted for having little to no upper wick, a lower wick which is at least twice the length of the candles body, and forming after a downtrend. It suggests a potential bullish reversal if confirmed by additional bullish candles.

Potential trade entry is on the next candle, if it remains bullish

This is a Reversal Pattern

Shooting Star Candlestick

A Shooting Star Candlestick has little to no lower wick, an upper wick that is twice the length of the body of the candle, and appears at or near the top of an uptrend. It suggests a potential bearish reversal depending of the price action that follows its close.

Potential Trade entry is on the next candle, if it remains bearish

This is a Reversal Pattern

Inverted Hammer Candlestick

An Inverted Hammer Candlestick has little to no lower wick, an upper wick that is twice the length of the body of the candle, and appears at the end of a downtrend. It suggests a potential bullish reversal depending if the candles that follow it are bullish.

Potential Trade entry is on the next candle, if it remains bullish

This is a Reversal Pattern

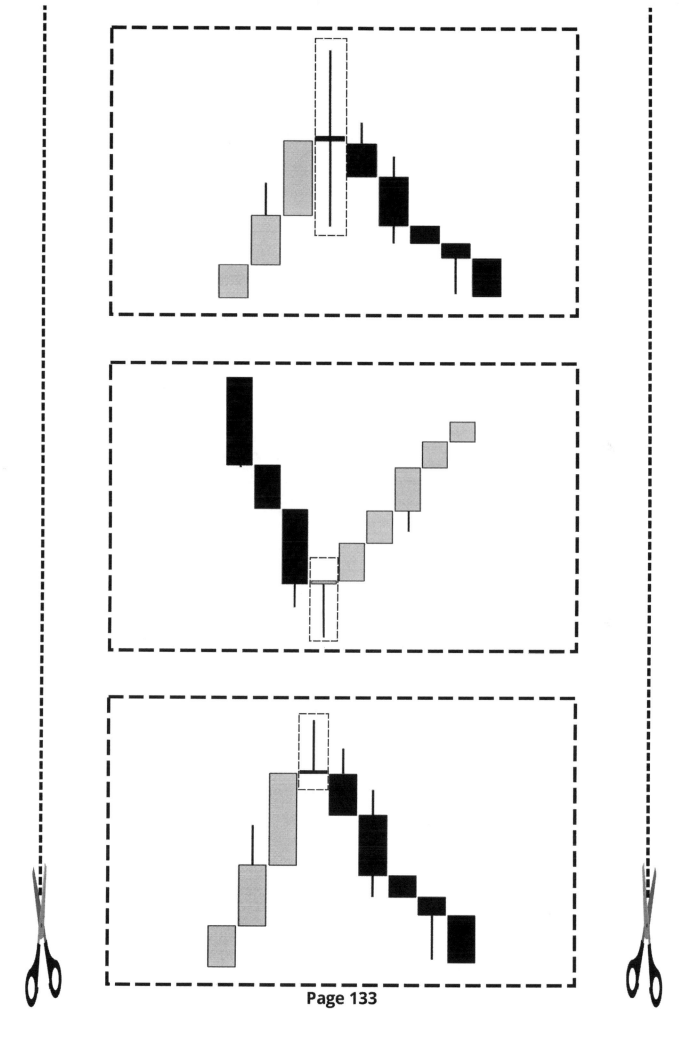

Doji Candlestick

The Doji Candlestick has almost no body with a varying length of upper and lower wicks, indicating that the opening and closing prices are very close or nearly the same. It represents market indecision and suggests a potential trend reversal. Traders look for confirmation from additional candlesticks to determine the direction of the next move.

**Potential trade enty is on the next candle,
if the next candle moves strongly in one direction**

This is a Reversal Pattern

Dragonfly Candlestick

The Dragonfly Candlestick is a Doji with little-to-no body or upper wick and a long lower wick. When at the bottom of a downtrend, this candlestick indicates a possible reversal. Traders look for confirmation from additional candlesticks before trading.

**Potential trade entry is on the next candle,
if that candle is moving up in price**

This is a Reversal Pattern

Gravestone Candlestick

The Gravestone Candlestick is a Doji with little-to-no body or lower wick and a long upper wick. When at the top of an uptrend, this candlestick indicates a possible reversal. Traders look for confirmation from additional candlesticks before trading.

**Potential trade entry is on the next candle,
if that candle is moving down in price**

This is a Reversal Pattern

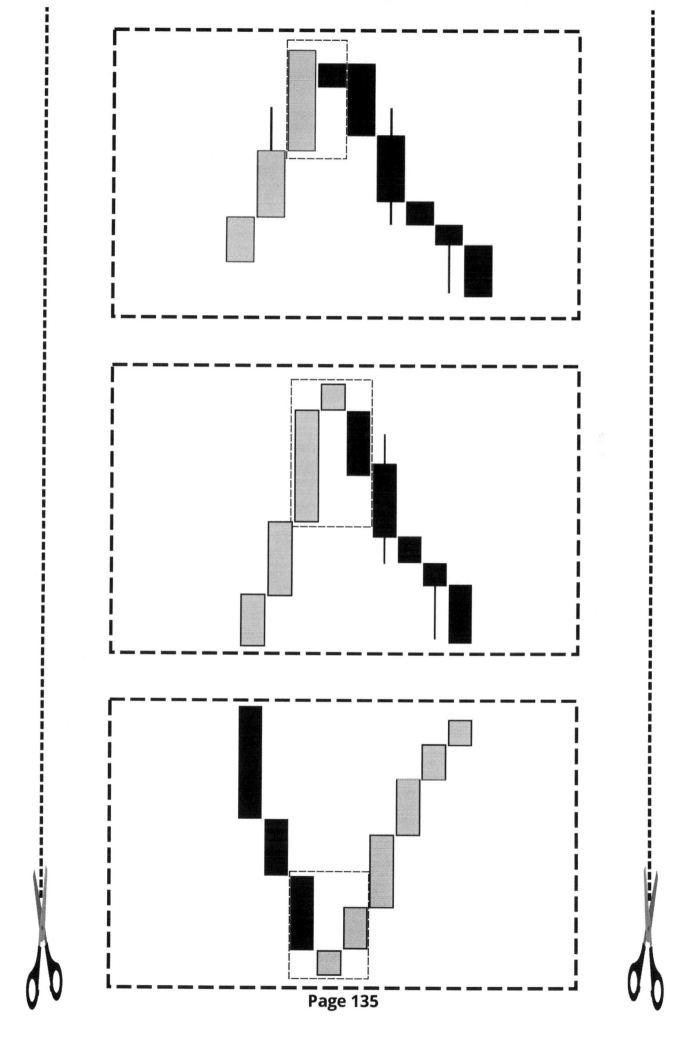

Bearish Harami Candlestick Pattern

The Bearish Harami Candlestick Pattern has two candles. The first candle is a long bullish candle. The second candle is a small bodied candle, its high and low are within the body of the first candle. The **close of the second candle** acts as a **support level.** Potential trade entry is when the price action breaks below the support level

This is a Reversal Pattern

Evening Star Candlestick Pattern

The Evening Star Candlestick Pattern has three candles. The first candle is a long bullish candle. The second candle is a small bodied candle. The final candle is a large bearish candle and closes near the middle of the first candle. The **close of the third candle** acts as a **support level.**
Potential trade entry is when the price action breaks below the support level

This is a Reversal Pattern

Morning Star Candlestick Pattern

The Morning Star Candlestick Pattern consists of three candles. First, a long bearish candle. Second, a small bodied candle. Third, a long bullish candle that opens above the second candle and closes near the middle of the first candle. The **close of the third candle** acts as a **resistance level.**
Potential trade entry is when the price action breaks above the resistance level

This is a Reversal Pattern

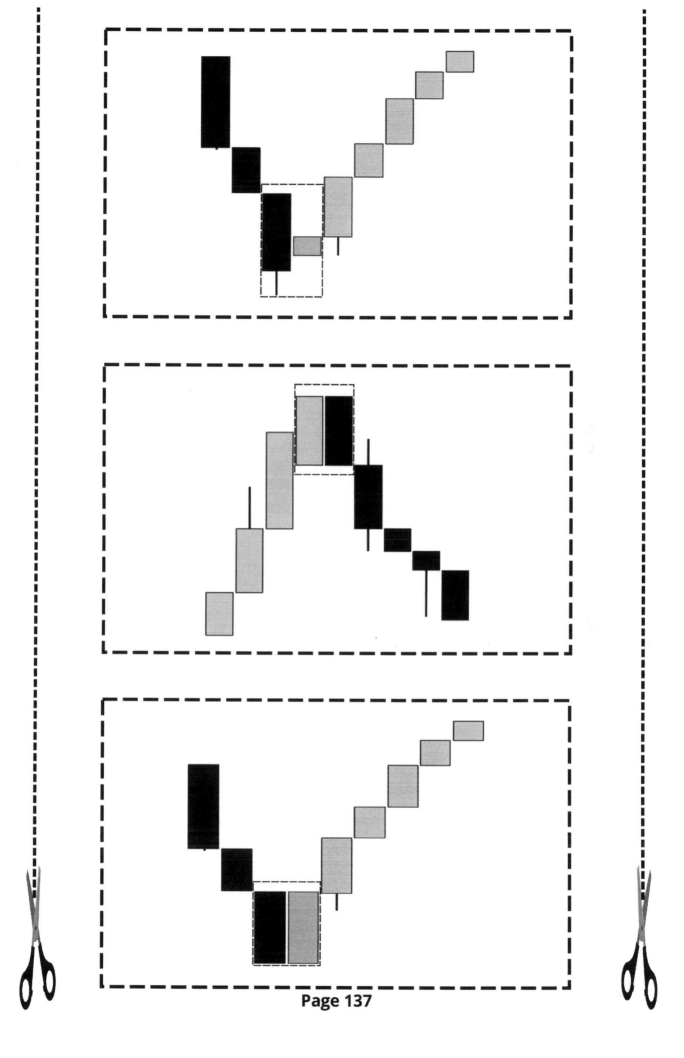

Bullish Harami Candlestick Pattern

The Bullish Harami Candlestick Pattern has two candles. The first candle is a long bearish candle. The second candle is a small bodied candle, its high and low are within the body of the first candle. The **close of the second candle** acts as a resistance **level.**
Potential trade entry is when the price action breaks above the resistance level

This is a Reversal Pattern

Bearish Tweezer Candlestick Pattern

The Bearish Tweezer Candlestick Pattern has two candles. The first candle is a long bullish candle. The second candle is a long bearish candle. Both candles have the same or nearly the same high price level. The **close of the second candle** acts as a support **level.**
Potential trade entry is when the price action breaks below the support level

This is a Reversal Pattern

Bullish Tweezer Candlestick Pattern

The Bullish Tweezer Candlestick Pattern consists of two candles. First, a long bearish candle. Second a long bullish candle. Both candles have the same or nearly the same low price level. The **close of the second candle** acts as a **resistance level.**
Potential trade entry is when the price action breaks above the resistance level

This is a Reversal Pattern

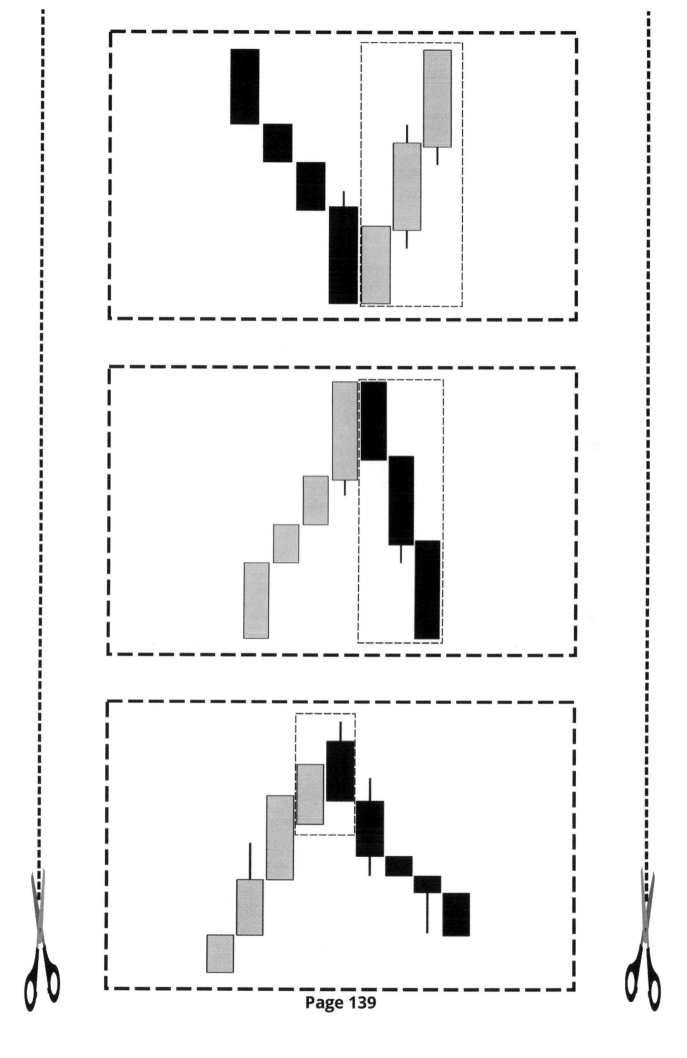

3 White Soldiers Candlestick Pattern

3 White Soldiers Candlestick Pattern has three candles. The three candles are long bullish candles, each opening within the body of the previous candle and closing above the high of the previous candle. The **close of the third candle** acts as a **resistance level**. Potential trade entry is when the price action breaks above the resistance level

This is a Reversal Pattern

3 Black Crows Candlestick Pattern

3 Black Crows Candlestick Pattern has three candles, each candle opening within the body of the previous candles and closing below the low of the previous candle. The **close of the third candle** acts as a **support level**. Potential trade entry is when the price action breaks below the support level

This is a Reversal Pattern

Dark Cloud Cover Candlestick Pattern

The Dark Cloud Cover Candlestick Pattern consists of two candles. First, a bullish candle. Second, a bearish candle that opens above the high of the bullish candle and closes more than halfway down the bullish candle's body. The **close of the second candle** acts as a **support level**. Potential trade entry is when the price action breaks below the support level

This is a Reversal Pattern

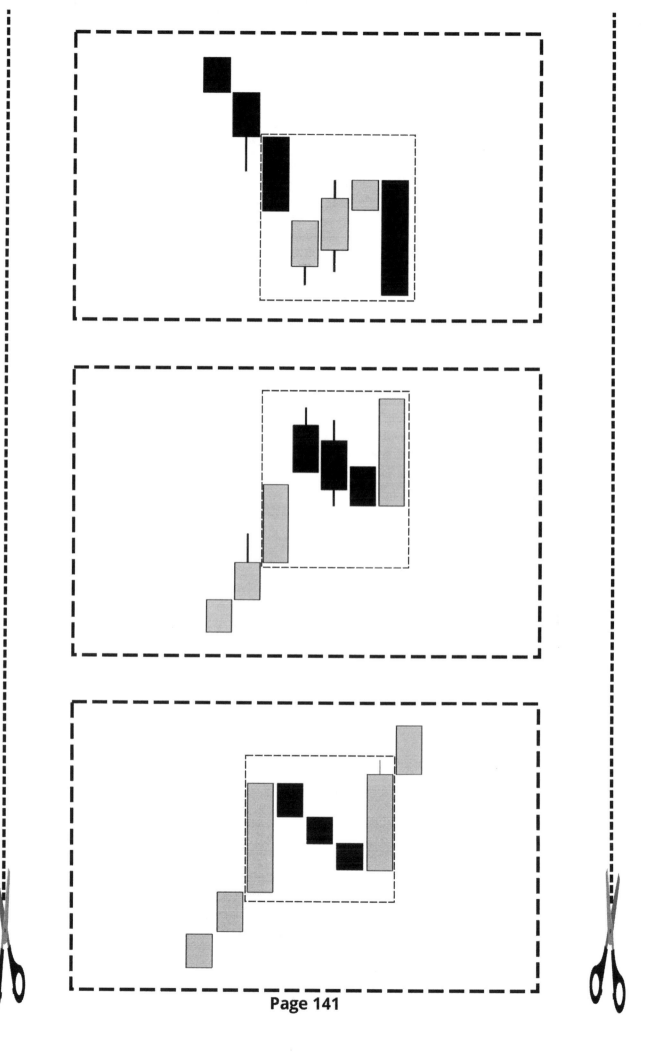

Bearish Mat Hold Candlestick Pattern

The Bearish Mat Hold Candlestick Pattern has five candles. The first candle is a long bearish candle. The second candle is bullish and opens above the first candle. Two more small bullish candles follow the second candle. The final candle is a long bearish candle that closes below the second candles low. The **close of the fifth candle** acts as a **support level**. Potential trade entry is when the price action breaks below the support level

This is a Continuation Pattern

Bullish Mat Hold Candlestick Pattern

The Bullish Mat Hold Candlestick Pattern has five candles. The first candle is a long bullish candle. The second candle is bearish and opens above the first candle. Two more small bearish candles follow the second candle. The final candle is a long bullish candle that closes above the second candle. The **close of the fifth candle** acts as a **resistance level**. Potential trade entry is when the price action breaks above the resistance level

This is a Continuation Pattern

Rising Three Candlestick Pattern

The Rising Three Candlestick Pattern consists of five candles. First, a long bullish candle, followed by 3 bearish candles that have highs and lows within the body of the first candle. The fifth is bullish candle that closes above all the other candles. The **close of the fifth candle** acts as a **resistance level**. Potential trade entry is when the price action breaks above the resistance level

This is a Continuation Pattern

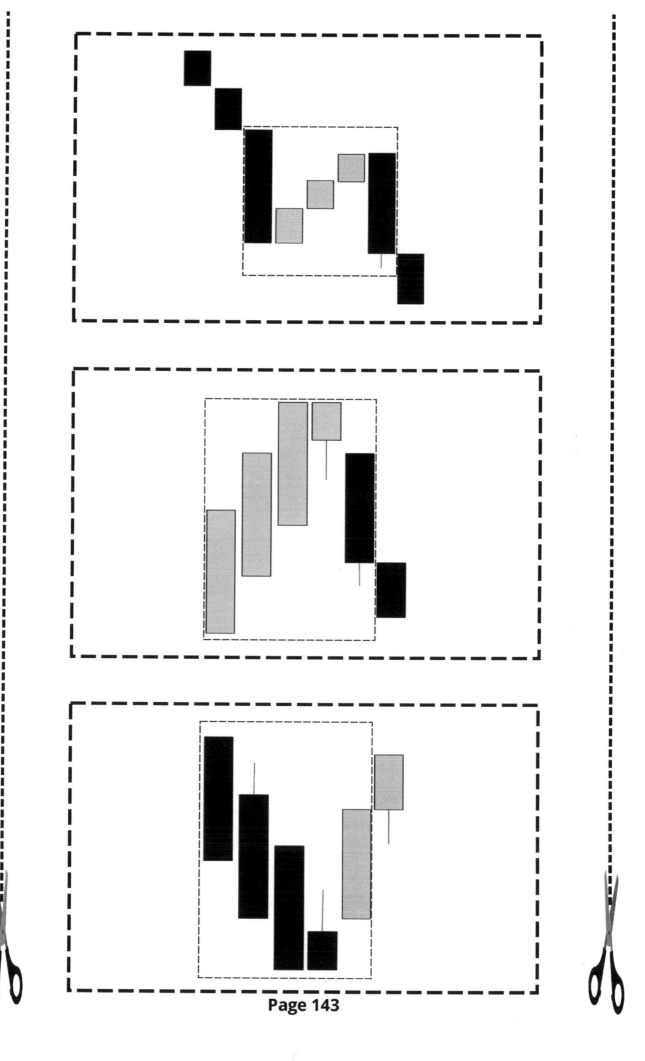

Falling Three Candlestick Pattern

The Falling Three Candlestick Pattern consists of five candles. First, a long bearish candle, followed by 3 bullish candles that have highs and lows within the body of the first candle. The fifth is bearish candle that closes below all the other candles. The **close of the fifth candle** acts as a **support level**.
Potential trade entry is when the price action breaks below the support level

This is a Continuation Pattern

Ladder Top Candlestick Pattern

The Ladder Top Candlestick Pattern has five candles. The first three candles are long bullish candles. The fourth candle is a bullish short bodied candle with a long wick. The fifth candle is a long bearish candle that opens below the body of the fourth candle. The **close of the fifth candle** acts as a **support level.**
Potential trade entry is when the price action breaks below the support level

This is a Reversal Pattern

Ladder Bottom Candlestick Pattern

The Ladder Bottom Candlestick Pattern has five candles. The first three candles are long bearish candles. The fourth candle is a bearish short bodied candle with a long wick. The fifth candle is a long bearish candle that opens above the body of the fourth candle. The **close of the fifth candle** acts as a **resistance level**.
Potential trade entry is when the price action breaks above the resistance level

This is a Reversal Pattern

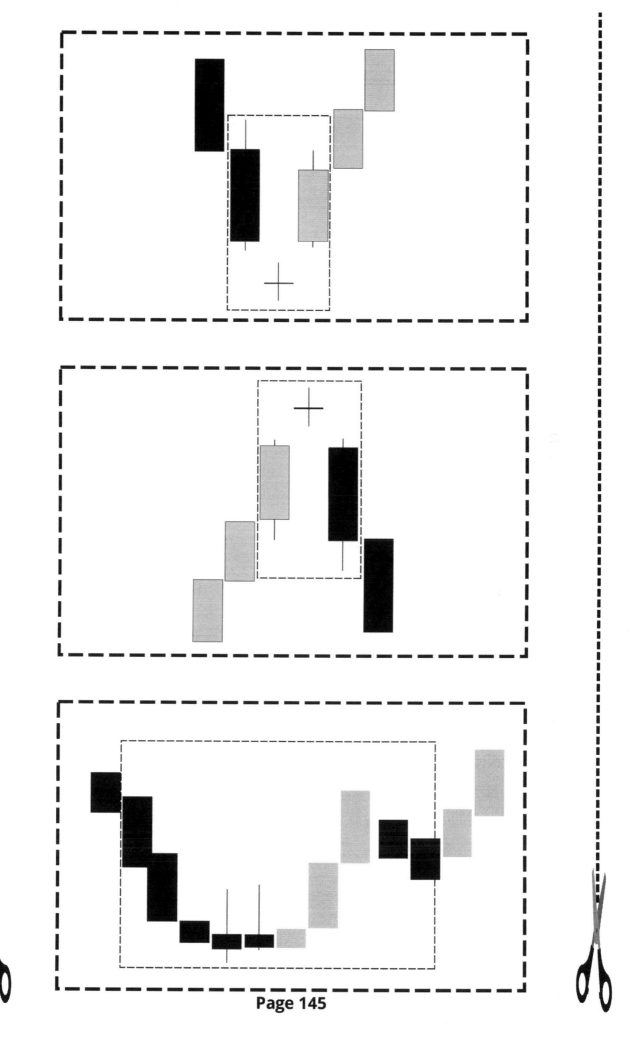

Page 145

Bullish Abandoned Baby Candlestick Pattern

The Bullish Abandoned Baby Candlestick Pattern has three candles. The first candle is a long bearish candle. The second candle is a doji candle that gaps below the first candle. The third is a long bullish candle that gaps above the second candle. The **close of the third candle** acts as a **resistance level.**
Potential trade entry is when the price action breaks above the resistance level

This is a Reversal Pattern

Bearish Abandoned Baby Candlestick Pattern

The Bearish Abandoned Baby Candlestick Pattern has three candles. The first candle is a long bullish candle. The second candle is a doji candle that gaps above the first candle. The third candle is a long bearish candle that gaps below the second candle. The **close of the third candle** acts as a support **level.**
Potential trade entry is when the price action breaks below the support level

This is a Reversal Pattern

Cup and Handle Candlestick Pattern

The Cup and Handle Candlestick Pattern is a bullish pattern. The "cup" is a U or bowl shape with lower volume as the candles form at the bottom. The "handle" is a pullback after the cup has formed. The handle is in consolidation. The highest part of the handle acts as a **resistance level.**
Potential trade entry is when the price action breaks above the resistance level

This is a Continuation Pattern

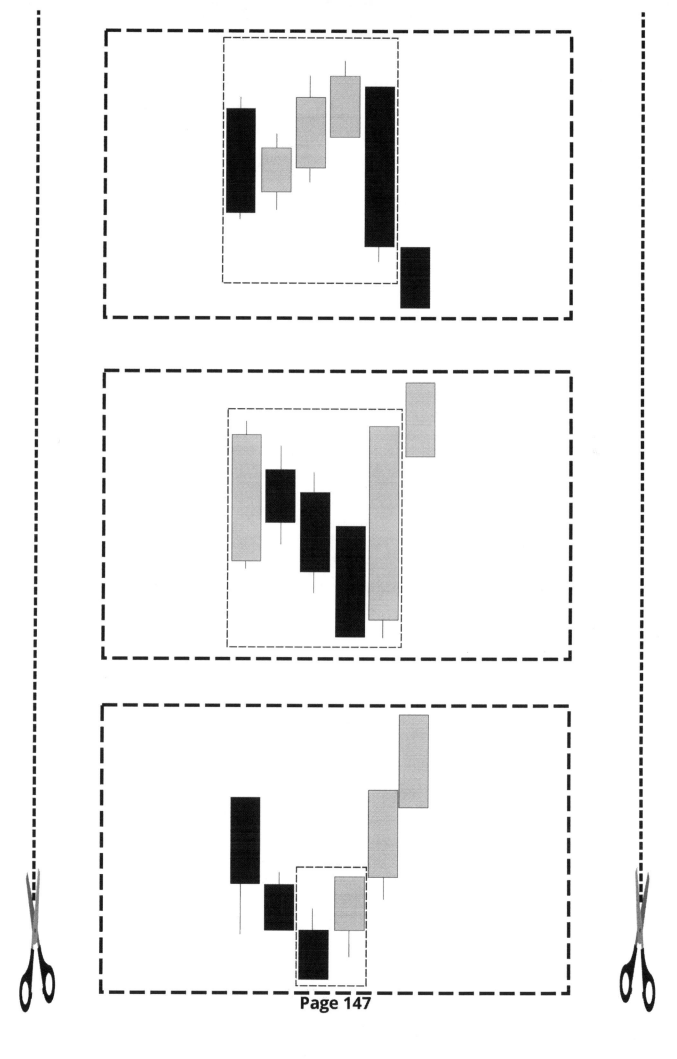

Page 147

Bearish Hikkake Candlestick Pattern

A Bearish Hikkake Candlstick Pattern is a 5 candle pattern. The first two candles form a Bullish Harami . The third and fourth candles are bullish candles that close higher than the previous candles. The final candle closes below the low of the second candle. The **close of the fifth candle** acts as a **support level**.
Potential trade entry is when the price action breaks below the support level

This is a Continuation Pattern

Bullish Hikkake Candlestick Pattern

The Bullish Hikkake Candlestick Pattern has 5 candles. The first candles form a Bearish Harami. The third and fourth candles are bearish that close lower than the previous candles. The final candle closes above the high of the second candle. The **close of the fifth candle** acts as a **resistance level**.
Potential trade entry is when the price action breaks above the resistance level

This is a Continuation Pattern

Bullish Separating Lines Candlestick Pattern

A Bullish Separating Lines Candlestick Pattern consists of two candles. The first candle is bearish and is followed by a bullish candle that opens at the same price level as the first candle opened. The high of the second candle acts as a **resistance level**.
Potential trade entry is when the price action breaks above the resistance level

This is a Reversal Pattern

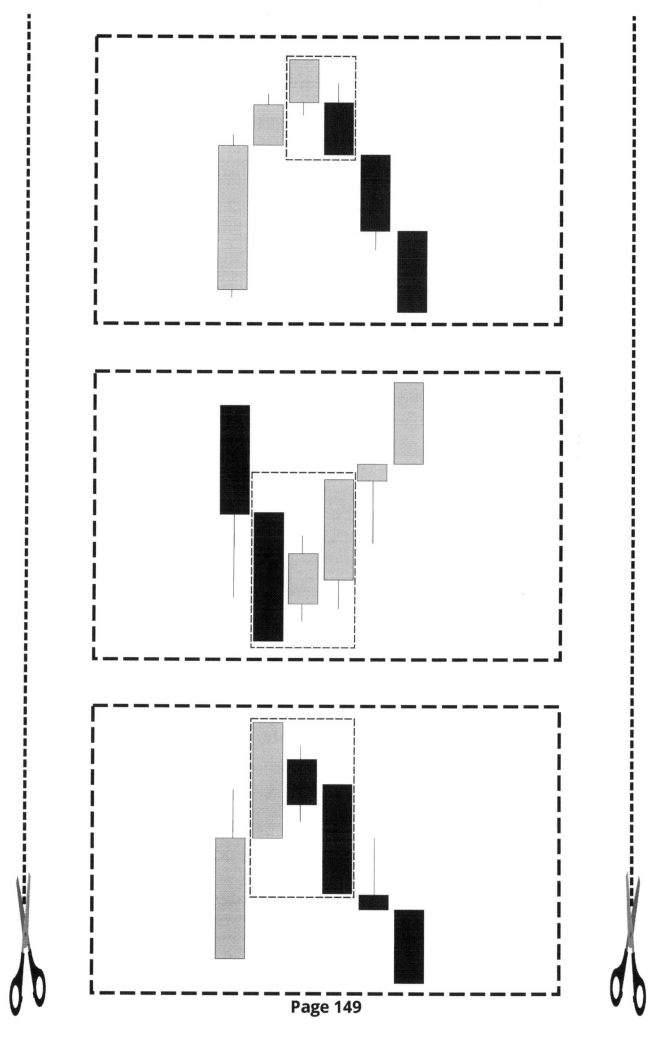

Bearish Separating Lines Candlestick Pattern

The Bearish Separating Lines Candlestick Pattern has two candles. The first candle is a bullish candle followed by a bearish candle that opens at the same price level that the first candle opened. The **close of the second candle** acts as a **support level**.
Potential trade entry is when the price action breaks below the support level

This is a Reversal Pattern

Three Inside Up Candlestick Pattern

The Three Inside Up Candlestick Pattern has three candles. The first candle is a long bearish candle; followed by a second, smaller candle, whose high and low price levels are between the open and close prices of the first candle. The third, a bullish candle, closes higher than the second candle.
The **close of the third candle** acts as a **resistance level**.
Potential trade entry is when the price action breaks above the resistance level

This is a Reversal Pattern

Three Inside Down Candlestick Pattern

The Three Inside Down Candlestick Pattern consists of three candles. The fist candle is a long bullish candle; followed by a second, smaller candle, whose high and low price levels are between the open and close prices of the first candle. The third, a bearish candle, closes lower than the second candle.
The **close of the third candle** acts as a **support level**.
Potential trade entry is when the price action breaks above the support level

This is a Reversal Pattern

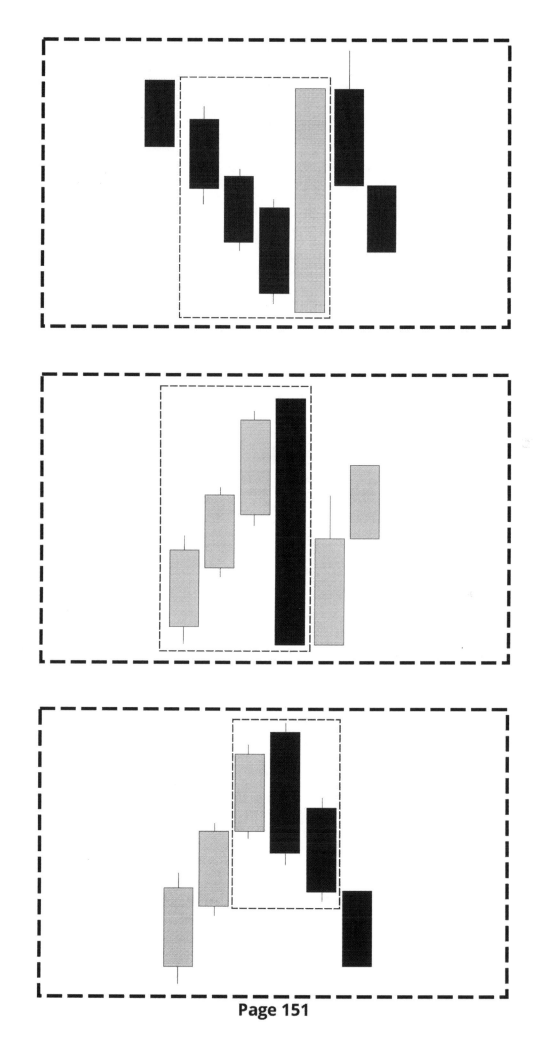

Page 151

Bearish Three Line Strike Candlestick Pattern

The Bearish Three Line Strike Candlestick Pattern has four candles. The first three candles are descending bearish candles that each open and close lower than the previous candles open and close price. The fourth candle is a long bullish candle that closes above the first candle's high. The **close of the fourth candle** acts as a **resistance level. Potential trade entry is when the price action fails to break the resistance level**

This is a Continuation Pattern

Bullish Three Line Strike Candlestick Pattern

The Bullish Three Line Strike Candlestick Pattern has four candles. The first three candles are ascending bullish candles that each open and close higher than the previous candle's open and close price. The fourth candle is a long bearish candle that closes below the first candle's low. The **close of the the fourth candle** acts as a **support level. Potential trade entry is when the price action fails to break below the support level**

This is a Continuation Pattern

Three Outside Down Candlestick Pattern

The Three Outside Down Candlestick Pattern is a three candle pattern where the first two candles form a Bearish Engulfing Candle and the third candle closes lower than the second candle. The third candle acts as a **support level**.
Potential trade entry is when the price action breaks below the support level

This is a Reversal Pattern

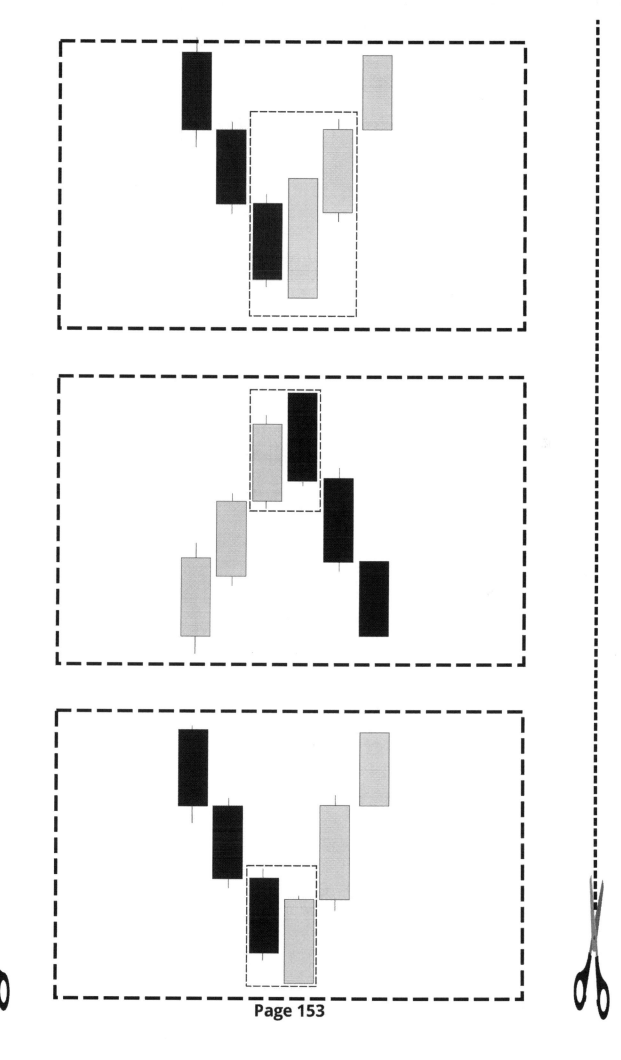

Three Outside Up Candlestick Pattern

The Three Outside Up Candlestick Pattern is a three candlestick pattern. The first two candles form a Bullish Engulfing Candle. The third candle closes higher than the second candle. The **close of the third candle** acts as a **resistance level.**
Potential trade entry is when the price action breaks the Resistance level

This is a Reversal Pattern

Bearish Belt Hold Candlestick Pattern

The Bearish Belt Hold Candlestick Pattern has two candles. The first candle is a long bullish candle and the second candle is a long bearish candle with little to no wick that opens higher than the previous candle's close. The **close of the second candle** acts as a support **level.**
Potential trade entry is when the price action breaks below the support level

This is a Reversal Pattern

Bullish Belt Hold Candlestick Pattern

The Bullish Belt Hold Candlestick Pattern has two candles. The first candle is a long bearish candle and the second candle is a long bullish candle with little to no wick that opens lower than the previous candle's close. The **close of the second candle** acts as a **resistance level.**
Potential trade entry is when the price action breaks above the resistance level

This is a Reversal Pattern

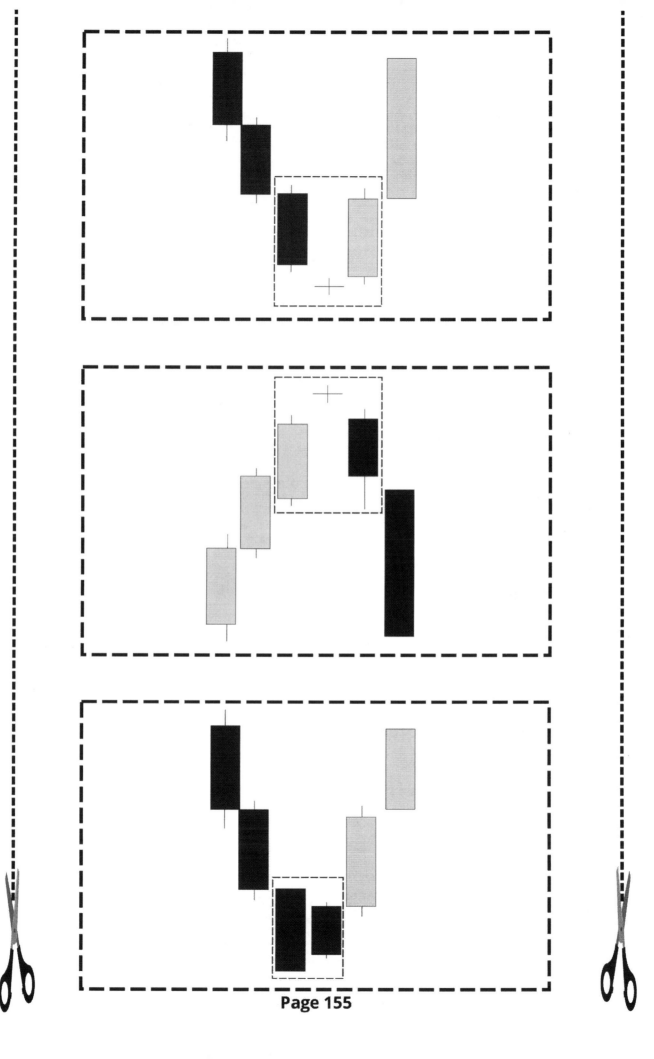

Bullish Doji Star Candlestick Pattern

The Bullish Doji Star Candlestick Pattern is a three candle pattern. The first candle is a long bearish candle. The second candle is a doji candle that opens and closes with a gap below the first candle. The third candle is a long bullish candle that closes above the midpoint of the first candle. The **close of the third candle** acts as a **resistance level**. Potential trade entry is when the price action breaks the resistance level

This is a Reversal Pattern

Bearish Doji Star Candlestick Pattern

The Bearish Doji Star Candlestick Pattern has three candles. The first candle is a long bullish candle. The second candle is a doji candle that opens and closes with a gap above the first candle. The third candle is a long bearish candle that closes below the midpoint of the first candle. The **close of the third candle** acts as a **support level**. Potential trade entry is when the price action breaks below the support level

This is a Reversal Pattern

Homing Pigeon Candlestick Pattern

The Homing Pigeon Candlestick Pattern has two candlesticks. The first candle is a long bearish candle. The second candle is a bearish candle with an open and closing price that fall inside the first candle's open and closing price. The **close of the 2nd candle** acts as a **resistance level**. Potential trade entry is when the price action breaks above the resistance level

This is a Reversal Pattern

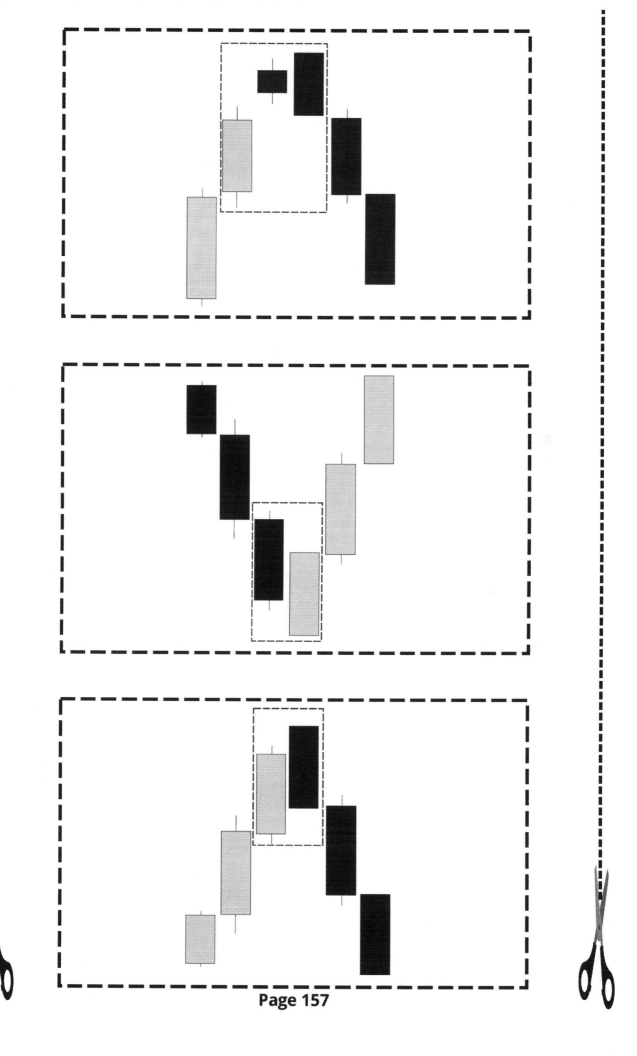

Page 157

Upside Gap Two Crows Candlestick Pattern

The Upside Gap Two Crows Candlestick Pattern is a three candle pattern. The first candle is a long bullish candle. The second candle is a bearish candle that gaps up and opens above the first candle. The third candle is a bearish candle that engulfs the second candle, but closes above the first candle's closing price. The **close of the third candle** acts as a **support level.**
Potential trade entry is when the price action breaks the support level

This is a Reversal Pattern

Bullish Piercing Line Candlestick Pattern

The Bullish Piercing Line Candlestick Pattern is a two candle pattern. The first candle is a bearish candle. The second candle is bullish and opens below the close of the first candle and closes above the midpoint of the first candle. The **close of the second candle** acts as a **resistance level. Potential trade entry is when the price action breaks below the resistance level**

This is a Reversal Pattern

Bearish Piercing Line Candlestick Pattern

The Bearish Piercing Line Candlestick pattern has two candles. The first candle is a bullish candle. The second candle is bearish and opens above the close of the first candle and closes below the midpoint of the first candle. The **close of the second candle** acts as a **support level**. **Potential trade entry is when the price action breaks above the support level**

This is a Continuation Pattern

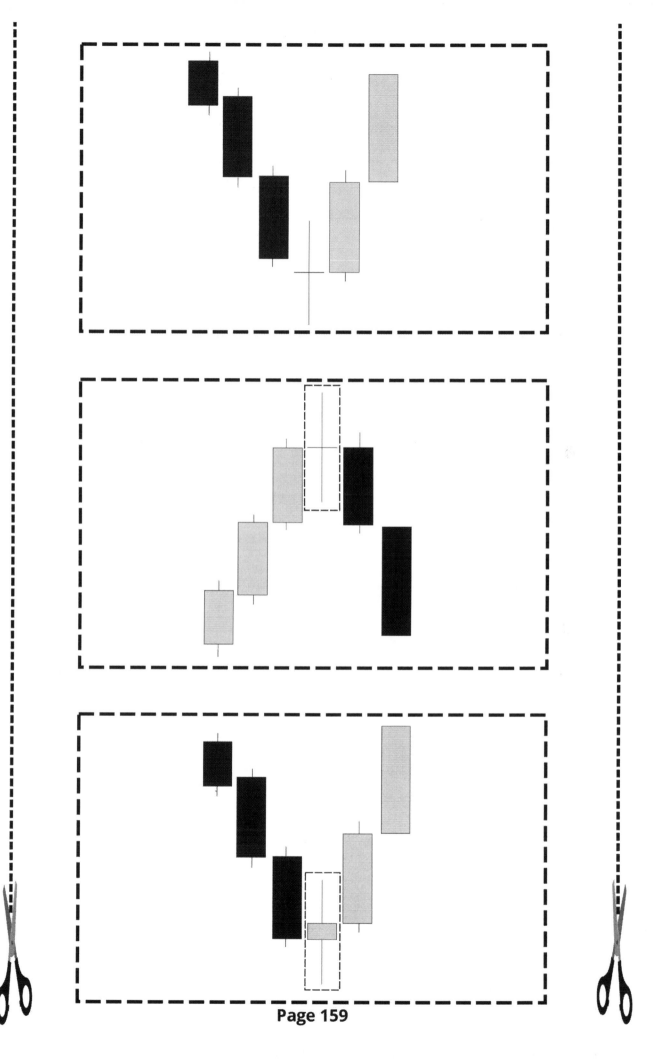

Bullish Rickshaw Man Candlestick Pattern

The Bullish Rickshaw Man Candlestick Pattern is a single doji candle characterized by an open and close that are nearly the same price and sit in the center of a long upper and lower wick and occuring at the end of a downtrend. The **high of the doji candle** acts as a **resistance level**. **Potential trade entry is when the price action breaks the resistance level**

This is a Reversal Pattern

Bearish Rickshaw Man Candlestick Pattern

The Bearish Rickshaw Man Candlestick Pattern is a single doji candle characterized by an open and close that are nearly the same price and sits in the center of a long upper and lower wick and occuring at the end of an uptrend. The **low of the doji candle** acts as a **support level.**
Potential trade entry is when the price action breaks below the support level

This is a Reversal Pattern

Bullish Spinning Top Candlestick Pattern

The Bullish Spinning Top Candlestick Pattern is a single candle with a small body between long high and low wicks. The **high of the candle** acts as a **resistance level**. **Potential trade entry is when the price action breaks above the resistance level**

This is a Reversal Pattern

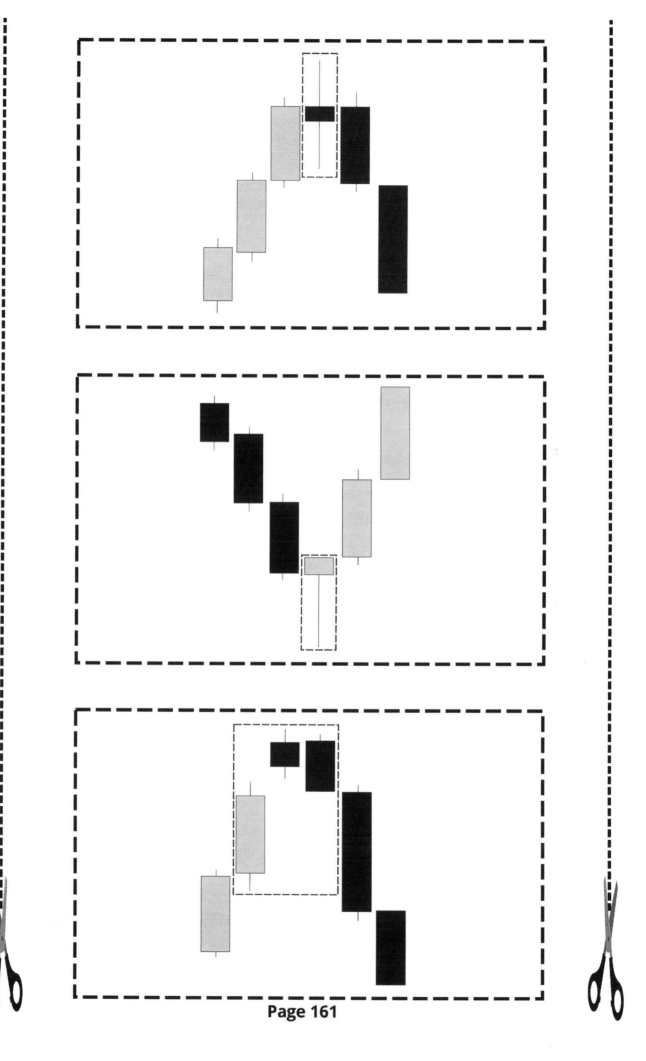

Bearish Spinning Top Candlestick Pattern

The Bearish Spinning Top Candlestick Pattern is a single candlestick that appears at the top of an uptrend characterized by a small body centered between long high and low wicks. The **low of the candle** acts as a **support level**.
Potential trade entry is when the price action breaks the support level

This is a Reversal Pattern

Takuri Candlestick Pattern

The Takuri Candlestick Pattern is a single candle that has a small body, with a lower wick that is 3 times the length of the body and no upper wick that is found at the bottom of a downtrend. The **high of the candle** acts as a **resistance level**.
Potential trade entry is when the price action breaks above the resistance level

This is a Reversal Pattern

Two Crows Candlestick Pattern

The Two Crows Candlestick Pattern is a three candle pattern. The first candle is a long bullish candle. The second candle is a bearish candle that gaps up from the first candle. The final candles is a long bearish candle that opens above the second candle and closes below the second candle, but above the first candle. The close of the third candle acts as a **support level**.
Potential trade entry is when the price action breaks below the support level

This is a Reversal Pattern

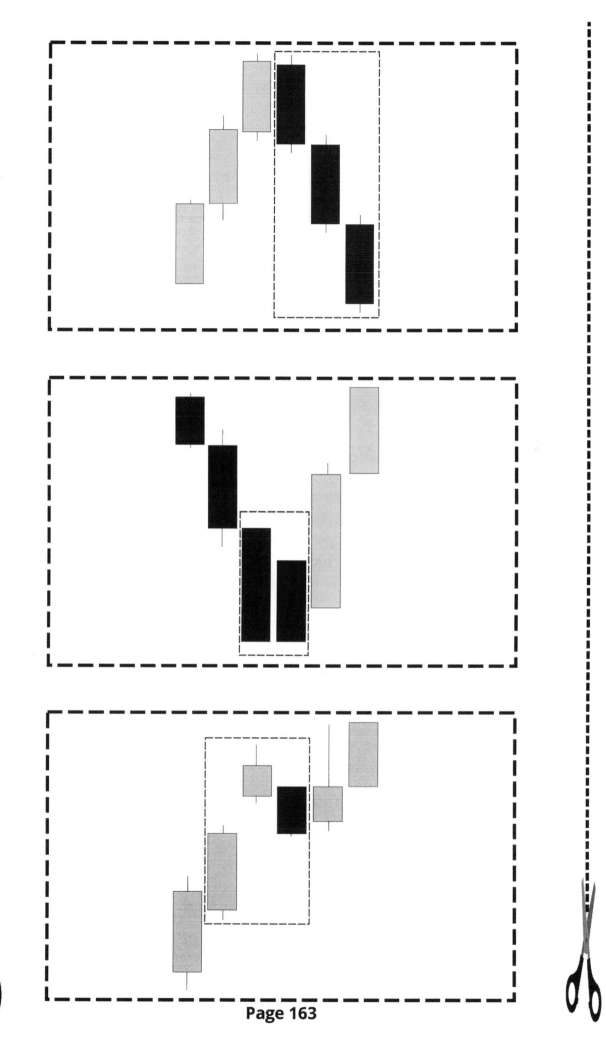

Page 163

Identical Three Crows Candlestick Pattern

The Identical Three Crows Candlestick Pattern is a three candle pattern. The three candles are long bearish candles of nearly the same price range. The **close of the third candle** acts as a support **level**.
Potential trade entry is when the price action breaks the support level

This is a Reversal Pattern

Matching Low Candlestick Pattern

The Matching Low Candlestick Pattern is a two candle pattern. The two candles are bearish and close at or very near the same price level. The **open of the second candle** acts as a **resistance level**.
Potential trade entry is when the price action rebounds from the resistance level and then passes the open of the second candle

This is a Reversal Pattern

Bullish Tasuki Gap Candlestick Pattern

The Bullish Tasuki Gap Candlestick Pattern has three candles. The first candle is a long bullish candle. The second candle is bullish and opens with a gap above the first candle. The final candle is bearish and partially closes the gap between the first and second candles. The open of the third candle acts as a **resistance level**.
Potential trade entry is when the price action breaks above the resistance level

This is a Continuation Pattern

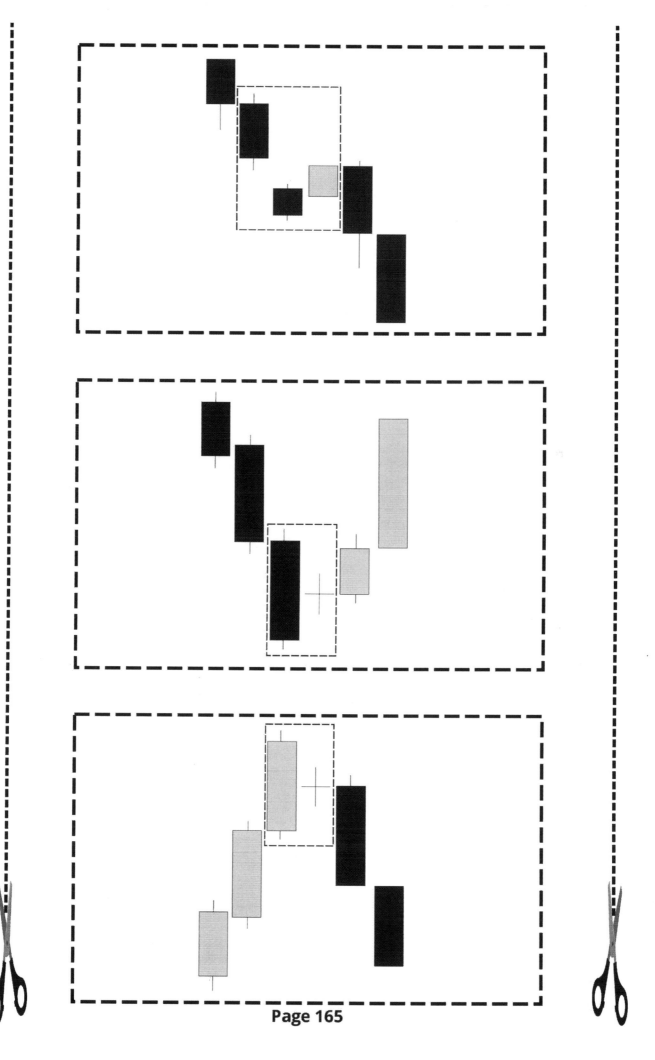

Bearish Tasuki Gap Candlestick Pattern

The Bearish Tasuki Gap Candlestick Pattern has three candles. The first candle is a long bearish candle. The second candle is bearish and opens with a gap below the first candle. The final candle is bullish and partially closes the gap between the first and second candles The **open of the third candle** acts as a **support level.**
Potential trade entry is when the price action breaks the support level

This is a Continuation Pattern

Bullish Harami Cross Candlestick Pattern

The Bullish Harami Cross Candlestick Pattern is a two candle pattern. The pattern is a Bullish Harami where the second candle is a doji. The **high of the second candle** acts as a **resistance level.**
Potential trade entry is when the price action breaks above the resistance level

This is a Reversal Pattern

Bearish Harami Cross Candlestick Pattern

The Bearish Harami Cross Candlestick pattern is a two candle pattern. The pattern is a Bearish harmi where the second candle is a doji. The **low of the second candle** acts as a **support level**.
Potential trade entry is when the price action breaks above the support level

This is a Reversal Pattern

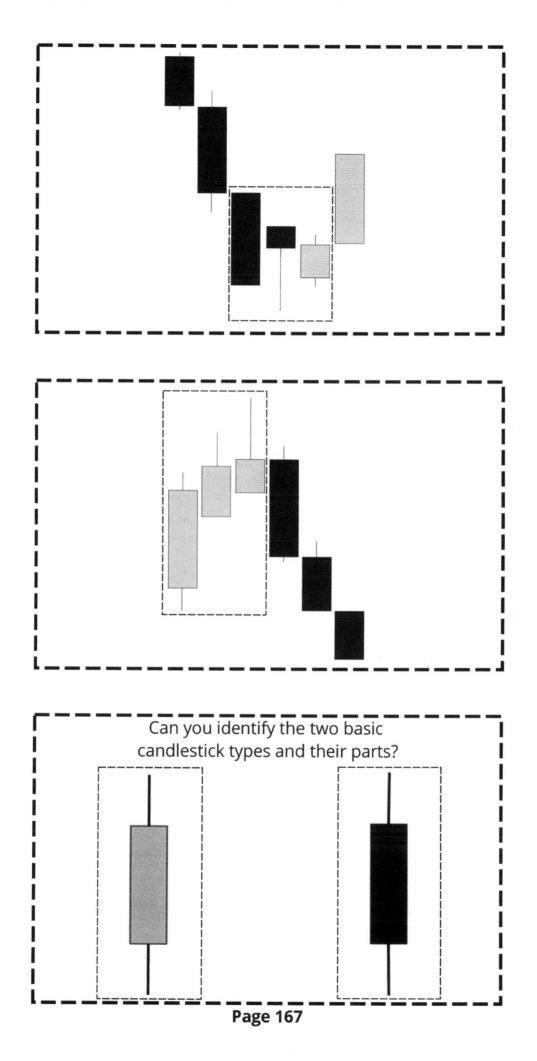

Can you identify the two basic candlestick types and their parts?

Page 167

Unique Three River Candlestick Pattern

The Unique Three River Candlestick Pattern has three candles. The first candle is a long bearish candle. The second candle is a hammer candle that makes a new low. The third candle is bullish and opens and closes within the high and low of the second candle. The **close of the third candle** acts as a **resistance level**. Potential trade entry is when the price action breaks above the resistance level

This is a Reversal Pattern

Advanced Block Candlestick Pattern

The Advanced Block Candlestick Pattern is a three candle pattern. The first candle is a long bullish candle. The next two candles are bullish and each has a smaller body and a longer wick than the previous candle. The **open of the third candle** acts as a support **level.** Potential trade entry is when the price action breaks below the support level

This is a Reversal Pattern

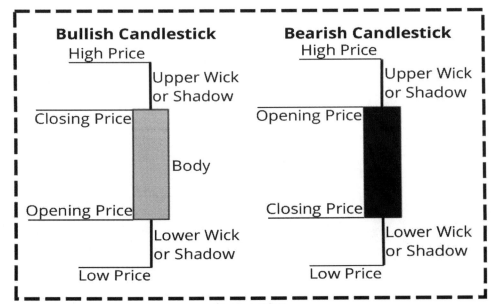

Stop Cutting Here!

Made in the USA
Las Vegas, NV
31 March 2024

88055416R00098